EXERCISES

AT THE

SEMI-CENTENNIAL

OF

AMHERST COLLEGE,

.

JULY 12, 1871.

SPRINGFIELD, MASS.:

SAMUEL BOWLES & COMPANY, PRINTERS.

1871.

AMHERST COLLEGE

SEMI-CENTENNIAL.

AT the annual meeting of the Alumni of Amherst College, July 8, 1868, the following resolutions were adopted:—

"*Whereas*, Our Alma Mater, in three years from now, will have completed her first half century, therefore,

"*Resolved*, That the Trustees of the College be requested to make provision for the celebration of that event.

"*Resolved*, That Professor William S. Tyler, D. D., be requested to prepare a history of Amherst College, which shall be ready for delivery at Commencement, 1871, and that he be requested also to address the Alumni on that occasion.

"*Resolved*, That a Committee of three be appointed to confer with the Trustees and with Professor Tyler, and to act as a Committee of Arrangements for our approaching semi-centennial."

In accordance with this last resolution, Professor R. D. Hitchcock, W. A. Dickinson, Esq., and Professor R. H. Mather, were appointed such a Committee, to whom, at the annual meeting of the Alumni, July 13, 1870, Professors Edward Hitchcock and J. H. Seelye were added.

At the annual meeting of the Board of Trustees, July 9, 1868, the foregoing action was approved and the Prudential Committee was authorized to confer with the Committee of the Alumni.

At the annual meeting of the Trustees, July 13, 1870, a special Committee, consisting of the President, Doctors Sabin,

Storrs and Paine, and Mr. Gillett, was appointed to make arrangements conjointly with the Committee of the Alumni for the celebration of the jubilee of the College in 1871.

After repeated meetings of the Committee of the Alumni by themselves, and conjointly with the Committee of the Trustees, the time and manner of the celebration were fixed as follows: The forenoon of Wednesday, July 12th, was assigned for the Address of Welcome by President Stearns, and the Historical Address by Professor Tyler. The afternoon of the same day was assigned for the Jubilee Meeting of the Alumni, while the evening was set apart for a social reunion of the Alumni and friends of the College.

The day came and passed auspiciously. The people of Amherst opened their hearts and homes with an unstinted welcome. Nearly seven hundred of the Alumni were present, representing every class, and coming from every quarter of the globe. A large tent for the public meetings was spread near the College grove, within which there were at least three thousand persons, besides many who stood around the open sides, or sat in their own carriages on the ground.

At the meeting of Wednesday forenoon, Hon. Samuel Williston fitly presided.

Rev. E. P. Humphrey of Louisville, Ky., led the assembly in the following prayer:

"O Lord, thou hast been our dwelling-place in all generations. Before the mountains were brought forth, or ever thou hadst formed the earth and the world, even from everlasting to everlasting, thou art God. For a thousand years in thy sight are but as yesterday when it is past.

"We thank thee, O God, that we are permitted to come here and now into thy presence, to call thee Our Father, and to address thee in prayer. We would begin with the petition which we are unworthy to offer, but which we would venture to urge, and be bold while we urge it, that thou wouldst forgive our many sins, for the sake of thy dear son our dear Saviour, and that thou wouldst bestow upon us the gift of the divine and eternal Spirit, to renew and sanctify our natures, and to prepare us for the rest that remaineth for the people of God.

"We would call upon our souls and all that is within us, to praise thee for the loving kindness in which we are assembled here. We thank thee now for what our eyes see and our ears hear, this day, of the favor which God Our Father has shown unto his servants who have labored at the foundations and in the upbuilding of this school of learning. We thank thee for the faith, for the courage, for the endurance, for the boldness, for the patience of those holy men who have gone before us in these many and mighty labors for the glory of God, and for the spread of the everlasting gospel throughout the world. For the liberality and zeal of those now living, who have entered into the labors here of those that have entered into the joy of the Lord, we thank thee. Bless all those to whom the affairs of this College are entrusted—the President, the legal Guardians, the Instructors and the Pupils. May they be taught of God.

"Bless us, thine unworthy servants, also, who received our training in this place for the spheres in which it has pleased thee to put us, in the Church, in the State and in human society. Help us in our lives and duties. May we show our gratitude to thee for what we have learned here, by employing ourselves with increasing diligence and growing love in the service of the Redeemer. And when we recall the names, and persons and gifts and graces of our classmates and fellow-students who have rested from their labors and have entered into the society of the saints made perfect—may we follow them as they followed Christ.

"Assist us, O Lord, as we proceed in these services. Guide

us and guard us and keep us as we sit together here, and rejoice together in the divine goodness. And as we hear the story of His blessed Providence, and his Almighty power and grace and mercy towards this Institution, through the age now closing upon us, may our hearts be lifted up in praise to God for the past, and in faith in his promises for the time to come. Great God! bless this College—bless it now, bless it evermore, and make it an enduring blessing. Help us to praise thee—help us to trust in thy mercy. May we attain unto the resurrection of the dead, and unto life everlasting. May we receive the crown of life; so that we may come into the presence of our Redeemer and cast each of us his crown at the feet of him that weareth many crowns.

"We ask all and offer all in the name of the Lord Jesus Christ, to whom with thee and the Holy Spirit we ascribe praise and dominion and power, forever. Amen."

The assembly then joined in singing the Doxology,

" Praise God from whom all blessings flow,"

after which followed the Address of Welcome by President Stearns, and the Historical Discourse by Professor Tyler.

PRESIDENT STEARNS' ADDRESS OF WEL-COME.

STANDING in the midst of this great congregation, still gathering together from far and from near for commemorations peculiar to scholars in the old mansion home of their literary birth and nurture, it is my privilege to express the gladness of the dear old mother as she throws the warm arm of affection around her great family of sons, and binds them again proudly and fondly to her heart.

Alumni of Amherst, *mater alma*, as she presents herself before you in matronly health and beauty on this fifty-year golden .wedding day of her espousals to all good learning and the motherhood of scholars, would look you all in the face, one by one, and altogether, and say from the depths of heart, welcome, welcome back again!

Alumni of Amherst, we welcome you this morning to the old College Hill, a spot once so familiar and never since forgotten ; to all you can recollect, to all you can enjoy. You come to us, many of you, after long and perhaps wearisome days of absence. You come from the midst of those life works and life struggles, which you could only anticipate when in college, but which now are serious realities to your experience. Let no thoughts of pulpit, or bar, or high places of state, or toils of teaching, or cares of business, or remembered sorrows, or hardships at hand, distract your attention from the duties and pleasures of the hour. We give the day to memory, to seeing, to enjoying. Memorials of the past may bring many things to mind, and views of the present furnish occasions for rejoicings. The old buildings, many of them, are here, and there are new ones which some of you have never inspected. There is Old South College, known by you all as the oldest college in the group, whose corner-stone was put down in singular faith, when almost nothing human justified the expectation that the top stone would ever be brought forth. There it stands, in the dignity of its time-honored plainness, solid, substantial, unfearing as its fathers who built it, and there you may see perhaps, to-night, what fifty classes have seen before you, all the windows of its many windowed-sides, finely set in their red brick frames, luminous and sparkling with the down-going sun, giving promise of glory all over it, as morrow after morrow returns upon it. And there stands the twin brother of it, what we now call North College, a second memorial of faith and works, perfecting each other. Some of you may find the apartments of these old dormitories which you used to occupy, and as you see in some of the closets, the mysteries of which you had better not inspect too minutely, the etchings and sketchings of more than one generation, you may learn that the sentiments and aspirations of students are essentially the same, as they were in your own college days. Step gently now about the room, for should you startle the echoes of all the voices, which have been heard therein from holiest psalm to jolliest song, you might be scared from your proprieties, and driven prematurely away.

And now the Old Chapel, built when the College was struggling for its charter, and embodying something of the idea—just behold it, from its western front,—meekly looking up, bravely looking out, patiently waiting for whatever may betide, there it stands between those two old dormitories like Moses between Aaron and Hur, the day that he fought the Amalekites. And the brave old tower, which the winds have rocked and swayed and shaken in many a tempest howling around it, but could never throw down, and the same old clock, which has been throbbing and striking and measuring out times for two thousand college lives, and the old bell or its successor, which has startled so many reluctant students from unfinished dreams, and rushed them, it is said, in olden times—some of you may remember them—half-dressed, and not half-awake, up the snow-covered hill before daylight, to the morning devotions, as they called it, and then to the tender mercies of unbreakfasted teachers, searching for knowledge where under such circumstances it was not likely to be found. But enter the building. Some of its apartments, though full of unsorted associations, strangely mixed up together, are yet redolent with the sweet blessedness which belongs to our religion, while most of them could tell stories of lesson-saying, some of which we might not care to remember. But, says the returning graduate of years back, "Oh, how changed,—nothing as it used to be." In the renovation of this old building a single room, just for your sake, has been left unimproved. There, under the guidance of the only classmate of one of you, the kindly tutor of some of you, the able professor of most all of you, hundreds of students have been introduced into the mysteries, the pleasures, and the despairs of the mathematics. You must see it—that well used old room, with its paper-hangings and its antique fittings, and the huge, long bench for apparatus, and the good professor behind it pouring light over the eyeballs of the seeing and the blind. We can not welcome you, to what used to be called the Old North College, in the medieval period of our college history. That great building, the largest, the most unsightly and most uncomfortable structure in the range, with wood and chips, and many other irregularities, under the snow around it, on a fearful night of snow-storm and hurricane, the thermometer many degrees

2

below zero, somehow caught fire, and ascended in a whirlwind
of smoke and flame to be dissipated in the heavens. So rapid
and terrible was the conflagration, bursting out everywhere,
raging like wrath which could not be appeased, that in three or
four hours, all the rooms of the building and all the timbers,
and boards and plastering and sheathing and roofing and walls
of it, with every living thing it contained, or which any one
had ever imagined it contained—all was destroyed, the students
only excepted.   1 seem to see them now, those frightened
men, some without hats, some without boots, some with beds
on their shoulders, some wrapped in great white blankets, as
they rushed like ghosts through the storm.   A photograph of.
the broken, blackened walls, taken some days after, now hangs
in the lower west room of the library, and is the only memorial
of one of the greatest catastrophies and one of the greatest blessings the College ever experienced.   Two new buildings sprung
up immediately from the ashes of the old, one of them, Williston
Hall, so comely in appearance, so convenient in arrangement,
so generously bestowed, and so full of invitation to the returning graduate as he comes up from the village to the college
grounds ; the other, East College, which the prophets represent
as destined to be taken down and rebuilt, or moved bodily to
another spot.

   We will not be betrayed into an enumeration or description
of all the college structures which you behold around you. But
as you go your rounds, you will wish just for a few moments to
notice the gymnasium and the power of systematic physical
training upon the young men who daily enjoy it.   And close
by is the new church, not yet completed, with its tower of
chiming bells, chiming not only for worship on Lord's day, but
chiming for our lamented braves who fell in the war, and the
memorial room consecrated to the service of Christian patriot-

ism, just beneath them, and the audience chamber of the Sabbath, where the students of many generations, free from the associations, and distractions of the week, can hear—

The old, old story of unseen things above,
Of Jesus and his glory, of Jesus and his love.

The greatest and most expensive of all our buildings is Walker Hall. You have heard of that old book,—" The Wonder-working Providence of Zion's Saviour in New England." There is hardly anything more wonderful in it than what Dr. Walker, a descendant of the author of it, has done for Amherst College. You must also look in upon the library and observe its overcrowded shelves and hear the grand old authors crying for room, and perhaps you can induce somebody to furnish means for its enlargement. Of course you will visit or revisit the cabinets ; some of them wonderful, some of them beautiful, all of them valuable, and for which Amherst College has been justly distinguished. We welcome you to the remembrance of the literary and other college societies, to the inspirations and exhilarations, the associates and the scenes of those dear old times, which will rush in upon you. Nor will you forget the society with its protracted and warlike appellation, which the department of hygiene and physical training has so assiduously cultivated for the promotion of health, sanity, scholarship and virtue. I know not whether the anti-veneneans are present in force, but I know that the great roll which contains the honored names of temperance men from the beginning has been sacredly preserved, and can be unfolded in its glory whenever you request it. Let successive classes make additions to it of men who have power to pledge, and the greater power to keep the pledge, till, when it may be unrolled some centuries hence, the parchment shall be too long for the town of Amherst or the county of Hampshire to contain it.

We welcome you to this old college homestead, marked out for it by the predestinating God who appointed the bounds of men's habitations before the foundations of the world.   People say we brag of our scenery! Why not? Is there anything more beautiful? The Holyoke range—how it rises like the walls of an immense cathedral wrought out by the genius of incomparable architecture, lifting its serrated summits to the firmament, supporting the great blue dome which arches over us and rests upon it and the mountains round about it.   And the silvery Connecticut, winding through intervales of surpassing loveliness, and Mount Tom, giant brother of great Holyoke, which the Almighty Worldbuilder in the far back times rent from it, that his beautiful waters, softly and sweetly flowing, might go through.   And the Pelham hills on the other side, animated with game, crowned with pines, fragrant with wild flowers in autumn.   Some of you will be thinking of the venerable Dr. Hitchcock in connection with these mountains.   You remember how he loved them, regarding them somehow as his own, and exercising dominion over them ; and how they acknowledged his supremacy ; and how, like Adam, next morning after creation, they came to him, or he went to them, and gave them names.   The classes specially concerned will never forget those new paths so suddenly extemporized over Holyoke and Norwottuck, and the greetings of celestials on the South Hadley side, nor the conflict of names between the Indian classic, Metawampe, and honest old Mount Toby—the College and the president on one side, and the good people of Sunderland in town meeting, resentful, on the other, and the resolutions that were passed by the contesting parties, —the whole affair constituting one of the most amusing passages in the history of the College—is it not all written in the book of Dr. Hitchcock's reminiscences? Nor will you forget the botany of Amherst, its ferns, and lichens, and flowers of every hue and every season, and the little garden which always blossoms in its innocence at the wrong time, and the Nubian Jungfrau which adorns it, and which, if not superior to criticism, is the best we can do. And the ornithology, every winged fowl after its kind, and especially the ancient crows on the Northampton road. "They live," it is said, "a hundred years." Some of them who were bravely cawing when Mr. Beecher used to chase them through the swamps and could not catch them, or when Professor Snell, then a stripling—God bless him, rehearsing in the woods the first commencement salutatory, bowed himself in the presence of these venerable aborigines and said, "Salutate omnes!" Some of them, ovantes in gutture corvi—cawing then, may be cawing still.

We welcome you also to the memory of representative men who represented the College before the public in days gone by, —its first president, Dr. Moore, the accomplished classical scholar, the kindly Christian gentleman, well known by six classes, though only two years in office, and loved by them all. With singular bravery of spirit, he undertook the founding of a College in the center of the commonwealth, and with faith and energy in the midst of discouragement, achieved what he undertook. Overworked and over-anxious he fell too suddenly, like the ox in the furrow, though not till the first plowing was completed and the sowing was well begun. Heman Humphrey took up the work. Twenty-three classes will remember him. Possessing the finest qualities of our New England ministry, it would have been difficult, if not impossible, to find another in all the ministry who could have been substituted for him. His position involved labor without sympathy, and endurance without commendation. He must be strong, though all around were weak, and furnish courage for many when there was no courage but in himself. With duties laborious, perplexing, embarrassing, with opposition from large portions of the public, and disheartening suggestions from many friends, that remarkable man, always working, always trusting, never pretending, wrought at the foundations of the College and above them, with an assiduity and perseverance never since surpassed. The venerable and kindly countenance, the resolved expression and majestic bearing, sobriety of manner, largeness of heart,— the man and his virtues will come to the recollection of many to-day. For myself, knowing what I do of his official position and the manner in which he sustained it, I am disposed to bow low and reverently in the presence of his memory, and in the view of the twenty-three years of his great working, say emphatically, " Servant of God, well done." Coming generations even more than ourselves, will acknowledge Heman Humphrey as chief of the chiefest in our earlier history. But there is no man so completely identified with Amherst College and prominent in the representation of it as its third president, Edward Hitchcock. Honored by all these classes, that benignant countenance, that large strong frame, the child-like sympathies and sensitive shrinkings, the faith that inspired great undertakings, and the lion-like courage, which, through misgivings of weakness, carried them forward to success, and that oft repeated prayer of his, that we might join at the last with the hundred and forty and four thousand in the great anthem above, will all be remembered. The embodiment of science for the Connecticut valley ; the foremost Christian geologist of his times ; the friend and father of successive classes of students, his grave still fresh with reverential tears, his foot-marks not confined to cabinets, but over all these grounds, his name will never cease to blossom on these hills and in the valley of the Connecticut so long as Amherst College shall endure.

Nor will you forget the good and distinguished men, who

were associated with the first three presidents, nor those who have taken up their work, and with all the powers that they possess, have been carrying it forward, hoping that One at least will recognize good endeavors and approve. Nor will any of you wish to pass by the hosts of our ascended. Some went as the yellow corn is gathered, when fully ripe, some like green ears, with their promise broken off, but let us be satisfied, for had they not finished the work which was given them to do? Those stars of the triennial! How they come out more and more thickly like a summer's night,—but as crowns of completed lives, thank God, they are stars of honor.

And the clangor of arms will be heard in your thoughts. You will remember the time when the drum-beat resounded, day and night, all over our states, and the everlasting tramp of our soldiery shook the land. Graduates and undergraduates, our beautiful boys in the silence of the night-watches, heard the bleeding country call them, and like a child when the mother cries, they could not be restrained. In the pride of young manhood, they went out,—resolve in the eye, glory in the soul, —and returned, many of them, no more. The time and the occasion forbid the flowing of too many tears, but perhaps the Mendelssohns will find opportunity out under the shades to offer up to them some tender requiem of remembrance and gratitude, and the chimes at twilight throw out a psalm or two upon the air, just to tell them how we loved them.

We welcome you to these dear old college grounds. They have undergone changes,—so have the grounds of all the advanced colleges,—which have made improvement. In consequence of the construction of new buildings, and the perversity of public demands, we can not make so beautiful a show as we could wish, at the moment. But if the earth about us still refuseth to be quiet, this is not because there are earthquakes beneath it, or convulsions threaten it, but, hopefully, because a new earth of permanence and beauty is expected to spring from it.

We welcome you, now, in conclusion, to our own homes and hearts; to the homes of our fellow-citizens, who have generously thrown open their doors to receive you; to a renewal of fellowship with us and with each other; to the memory of the many things you enjoyed and the few things you suffered in your college course; to the opening up of the past with story and sympathy and song; to the hearing of good speeches, some well considered and weighty, some sparkling and extempore, no one forgetting that "brevity is the soul of wit," and that even "linked sweetness long drawn out," on an occasion like this, is intolerable. We wish to make you happy, as when children come home to Thanksgiving. And if, in the crowd and rush of the day, our arrangements should seem inadequate, no one will be so sorry as Alma Mater, that a single son should feel neglected. Welcome, then, once more, welcome to our jubilant festivity, and welcome to inspirations rising up to a working enthusiasm for the future of the College; and, with strong prayers to the Almighty, welcome to a jubilant launching of the old ship on her second half-century voyage, to return again when the hundred year clock shall strike one, loaded with treasures of good deeds accomplished, and hailed on its landing with the jubilee psalms of thousands of consecrated scholars, and the grateful Amens of the whole earth.

PROFESSOR TYLER'S HISTORICAL AD-DRESS.

Mr. President, Brothers of the Alumni, Trustees and Friends of Amherst College:

FIFTY years ago on the 18th of September next, the South College and the Fifty Thousand Dollar Charity Fund, which were all that then existed of Amherst College, were solemnly dedicated to the service of God and "The great Head of the Church." At the same time, President Moore and Professor Estabrook, having publicly assented to a confession of faith prepared for the purpose, were inaugurated into their respective offices. There were two other Professors elect, Rev. Gamaliel S. Olds and Rev. Jonas King; but Professor Olds was unavoidably absent, and Mr. King soon after went as a missionary to Greece, and never accepted the Professorship. The exercises of this occasion were held in the Old Parish Meeting-house, which stood on the site then, and ever since known as Meeting-house Hill. Noah Webster, Esq., presided as President of the Trustees of Amherst Academy, under whose auspices the College commenced its existence. The incumbents were appropriately charged with their sacred trust by the President of the Board, and they, in turn, delivered brief inaugural addresses. Prayers were offered by Rev. Mr. Crosby of Enfield, Vice-President of the Board, and Rev. Mr. Snell, pastor of the church in North Brookfield. A sermon was preached by Rev. Dr. Leland of

3

Charleston, S. C., Professor Stuart of Andover Theological Seminary, who had been appointed to preach on the occasion, and Rev. Mr. Osgood of Springfield, his substitute, having both failed to fulfil their appointments. The text was, " On this rock will I build my church, and the gates of hell shall not prevail against it." At the close of the exercises, the corner-stone of the president's house was laid with appropriate ceremonies.

The next day, September 19, 1821, forty-seven students were examined and admitted, some to each of the four classes. The first student who was admitted to the institution, and the only one who was admitted on the forenoon of that day, entered the senior class. He is now our oldest, and, it is no flattery to add, our most loved and honored Professor. Well may he look back to that day, and as modestly and gratefully as truly say, " Magna pars fui,"— nay, so far as students were concerned, he was for some hours the whole of Amherst College. Fortunate man, whose life as a scholar and an educator thus runs parallel with the life of the College, and who, for one year of imperfect training, has requited his alma mater with almost fifty years of the clearest and most exact, and, in many respects, the wisest and best instruction, that has ever been given within these walls.

All who took any part in the first day's exercises have long since ceased to mingle with earthly scenes,[*] and the building in which the services were held, has given place to others. All the officers and a majority of the students who participated in the examinations of the second day, are starred on our catalogue, and, we trust, shine as stars in the heavenly sphere. But the institution which then commenced its existence, and whose fiftieth anniversary we are now convened to celebrate, lives, and will live, (we trust in the faithfulness of a covenant-keeping

---

[*] Since the delivery of this address I have learned that Dr. Leland is still living.

God,) through thousands of generations of officers and students who fear Him and keep His commandments.

In comparison with the long and ever increasingly prosperous future, which, we hope, awaits our beloved College, the half century that has elapsed is but a day, and a day of small things. Relatively, also, to older institutions, which reckon their duration not by years or decades of years, but by centuries and ages, a semi-centennial seems scarcely worthy of celebration. As the traveler in the old world visits Oxford, for example, founded (or revived, antiquarians are not agreed which,) by the good King Alfred a thousand years ago, and walks through the gates, quadrangles, cloisters and libraries of its numerous colleges and halls, which have been accumulating their educational resources and their sacred memories of great men ever since the university was founded, and sits down to meditate under the shadow of the trees where Wickliffe and Wolsey and More and Raleigh, Hampden and Hale and Locke and Blackstone have perchance sat before him, and successive generations of yet earlier scholars and distinguished men, who studied there centuries before the discovery even of the continent in which we live—in the view of such a traveler our College and the half century of its existence dwindle and sink into comparative insignificance. As he passes on to Rome, whence the nations of modern Europe and America all derived their civilization, and visits Athens, whence the Romans received their literature and science, and the moderns their art and culture,—as he goes up to Jerusalem, whose mission it was to teach the world religion, and especially, when he comes to Egypt, where Romans, Greeks and Jews all went to school in the primitive ages—where forty centuries looked down from the pyramids upon the army of Napoleon, and where some Egyptologists imagine that a hundred centuries look down upon them—in such a presence, he

may be pardoned if he begins to feel that a half-century celebration is not only a small affair, but an absurdity and almost
an impertinence.   But in Egypt, the earth is as silent and fixed
as the heavens, and society as unchanging as nature herself;
and a half century perchance effects greater social and educational changes in our country than are brought about there in
the lapse of ages.

Even England is slow and immovable in comparison with
America, for, as the first minister of Salem, Rev. John Higgin-
son, said, "A sup of New England aire is better than a whole
draught of Old England's ale," and we build colleges and other
institutions as we do houses, doing in a few days what would
there be the work of months or years, and finishing (so far as
we finish anything) in a few years, what would there be the
growth of centuries.   But this activity of the new world is re-
acting upon the old world, and introducing *there at length* an
element of change, reform and progress, in place of the old im-
mutability.   A century has not yet elapsed since the foundations of our federal government were laid.   Yet our revolution
is one of the principal causes that have revolutionized Europe,
reaching to Rome, to Athens, to Egypt, nay, even to China and
Japan.

And although it is only half a century since Amherst College was opened for the reception of students, its influence in
education and religion is already felt, not only through the
United States, but in every quarter of the globe.   It is not, then,
arrogance and presumption—it is simple justice, nay, it is a
sacred duty that we should assemble, as we have to-day, from
every part of our land and every part of the world, to honor
the memory of those who have laid these foundations, and, at
the same time, to revive the sacred recollections and associations of our own residence within these walls.

It is not easy to measure or comprehend the changes that have passed over our country and the world during the last half century. Fifty years ago, the population of these United States was between nine and ten millions. Now it is nearly forty millions, having almost quadrupled during the half century. Then there were twenty-four states ; now there are thirty-seven. Fifty-one years ago, Missouri, the first state which lies wholly west of the Mississippi, was received into the Union. Now there is a strenuous effort to remove the capital to St. Louis, and even that is hundreds of miles east of the center. Then we had a million and a half of slaves. Now slaves can not breathe the air of the United States, and the influence of this stupendous revolution in our country has sealed the doom of slavery in South America and the West India islands, and of serfdom in Russia and every part of the old world. Then we had but recently closed an ineffectual war with Great Britain, leaving the questions in dispute just as they were before the war began. The recently ratified treaty of Washington, by the acceptance of American principles of international law, and by the reference of all minor differences to arbitration, has not only re-established amicable relations between Great Britain and the United States without an appeal to arms, but inaugurated a new era in the history of nations—the era of friendly arbitration instead of bloody and cruel war—the era, it is hoped, of peace on earth and good will among men, destined, ere long, to become universal.

Just half a century ago, the first Napoleon, then a prisoner at St. Helena, uttered that remarkable prophecy, " In fifty years Europe will be either Republican or Cossack." This prediction has not been fulfilled either in the letter or in the bitterness of his disappointed and sarcastic spirit. But Europe is now governed by the voice of the people, whatever may be the form of the government or the title of the rulers; and Russia, the friend and ally of the United States, and Prussia, the great Protestant power of Europe, divide the hegemony, the virtual sovereignty between them; while the Catholic powers, France, Spain and Italy, instead of establishing a Latin empire in America, are fain to settle disputed questions of government and policy by the American principle of popular suffrage. Fifty years ago the sovereigns of the miscalled Holy Alliance were lording it over Europe, and disposing of cities and nations as they pleased, in the interest of despotism. Now a Holy Alliance of peoples and nationalities, constituted by nature and the providence of God, dispose of kings and emperors at their sovereign will in behalf of liberty and humanity. In 1825, at the semi-centennial celebration of the battle of Bunker Hill, Lafayette said, "Bunker Hill and the holy resistance to tyranny have already enfranchised the American hemisphere; the next half-century jubilee toast shall be to enfranchised Europe" There is time enough between this and 1875 for this prophecy, already so nearly fulfilled, to be fully accomplished.

Half a century ago, there was not a mile of railway for the transportation of passengers and merchandise anywhere in existence. Now there are fifty thousand miles of railway in the United States, which have cost two thousand millions of dollars, whose annual earnings exceed four hundred millions— more than the whole valuation of the country fifty years ago. The older alumni will hardly need to be reminded of their long rides, early and late, perhaps till midnight, in the old stage-coach to Boston, or Hartford, or Albany, perchance to far greater distances. Nor will the later graduates soon forget their hair-breadth escapes and break-neck experiences in the same lumbering vehicle between Amherst and Palmer, Brookfield or Northampton. In one instance, I well remember, a tipsy driver upset the whole dignity of the College, and over-turned the Government, Trustees, President and all, in driving down the hill this side of Belchertown.

The Pacific railroad is the modern wonder of the world. It has reversed the currents of travel and trade, and reduced immensely the circumference of the globe. Formerly the shortest way from New York to Canton was via London; now the quickest route from London to Canton is via New York. Then, without steamships or telegraphs, passengers and news were from twenty to sixty days in crossing the ocean, according to the wind and weather. Now passengers cross in little more than a week, while intelligence is transmitted almost instantaneously, and the same news from every part of the world is read the same day, perchance the same hour and moment, on both sides of the Atlantic.

Fifty years ago, men talked and wrote of the power of the press very much as we do now. But the daily newspapers in Boston, New York and Philadelphia were then quite content with a circulation of two thousand copies—three or four thousand was their highest aspiration. No one of the monthly and weekly magazines, which are now expected with so much interest by almost the whole population, was then in existence. And if the men and women of that day had been told that the time would ever come when a newspaper would strike off a hundred thousand copies in a single morning, or a magazine would have a circulation of half a million, they would have pronounced the man insane who ventured to utter such a prediction. Our review literature began with the North American in 1815, and our religious newspapers with the Boston Recorder in 1816,—just about the time Amherst Academy came into existence, and only five years before the foundation of Amherst College. They read books in those days, especially one book, the Bible. Now

the masses scarcely read anything but magazines and newspapers. Then there was such a thing as privacy and retire-
ment. Now everybody does everything in the sight of the
whole civilized world.

When Amherst College was founded, there was neither gas-
light nor petroleum. Gas-light was first introduced into Boston in 1822, and the students of Amherst continued to read
their Greek text and trace their mathematical diagrams in the
light of an oil-lamp, or in the darkness of a tallow candle,
through more than three-fifths of the half century, till, by human
skill and the providence of God, oil gushed out of the rock, and
there was both physical and intellectual light.

The educational institutions of the country were then in their
infancy, imperfectly manned, poorly furnished, and scarcely at
all endowed, as little developed comparatively as the facilities
for light and locomotion. In 1821, Yale College had five professors and six tutors; Harvard, in her academical department,
had scarcely more. Four hundred pounds—eight hundred at
most—was the sum which Harvard received from the benefactor
whose name it bears. Yale College received five hundred pounds
from Governor Yale. Lord Dartmouth gave only fifty guineas
to Dartmouth College. The day had not yet come when wealthy
and benevolent men would give a hundred thousand dollars, or
a quarter or a half million, and that to institutions not bearing
the name of the donor. College buildings were then all after
one pattern—whether it resembled more the barrack or the
prison, it were not easy to say; and the course of study was
stereotyped, one and the same in all the colleges, and almost the
same which had existed for several generations. Greek, Latin
and mathematics, six times a week, with a little natural philosophy at the end, and perhaps a little rhetoric and logic in the
middle, was the curriculum for the first three years, and mental

and moral philosophy, with a sprinkling of theology and political economy, was the course for the fourth year. The Graeca Minora was the Greek required for entering, and the Graeca Majora was the Greek studied after admission in every New England college, and I doubt not in every college in the United States. Chemistry, mineralogy, geology, zoology, paleontology, and the other ologies had not yet begun to distract the minds of students; and laboratories, museums, cabinets, collections in natural history, were to be the growth of the next half century. The idea of a university with studies wholly elective, for boys fresh from the farm and the shop, or, at best, just out of the high school and the academy, had not yet dawned upon the darkened minds of presidents and professors, or even of the most progressive sophomores and freshmen. High schools were comparatively few even in Massachusetts. Academies were springing up rapidly in the larger towns, and theological seminaries were just coming into existence. Young men had hitherto fitted for college, and studied divinity chiefly under the instruction of such pastors as Dr. Backus and Dr. Hooker of Connecticut, and Father Hallock of Plainfield, Dr. Morse of Charlestown, and Dr. Emmons of Franklin, in Massachusetts.

But the decade of years which preceded the founding of our College was a period of great political, mental, moral and religious activity. It was during this period that the Spanish populations of Mexico and South America threw off the yoke of the mother country, and declared their independence. The republics of Mexico, Columbia and Peru all commenced their separate political existence in 1821. The Greek revolution also broke out the same year in which our College was opened; and within ten or twelve years, there were young Greeks from more than one of the fabled birthplaces of Homer in nearly all our College classes. These political revolutions, inaugurating a new

4

era in both hemispheres (in the hopes at least of young and ardent minds), and opening a new and vast field of enterprise to the friends of liberty, humanity, learning and religion, were attended by corresponding movements in the moral and religious world. It was during this same decade that Bible societies sprang up all over Europe, and most of our great missionary societies in America, together with other kindred associations, had their origin. The American Board of Commissioners for Foreign Missions was established in 1810, the American Education Society in 1815, and the American Bible Society in 1816. It was not till 1826 that the American Home Missionary Society and the American Temperance Society came into existence. The theological seminary at Andover was established in 1808, the seminary at Princeton in 1812, and that at Auburn in 1819. The Yale Divinity School will celebrate its semi-centennial next year.

The twenty years between 1815 'and 1835, are often spoken of as distinguished above any period of equal length in modern times, for the frequency, purity and power of the revivals of religion which then prevailed; and of the years in this distinguished period, with the exception of 1831, 1821, the year in which our College was founded, was perhaps, beyond all others, emphatically a year of the right hand of the Most High. The wars of Napoleon had now come to an end, and the nations were at rest and at peace. Our own war with Great Britain—always to be known, I trust, as our "last war" with the mother country—had also ceased, and the Christian community now awoke to a new spiritual life, and consecrated their energies and resources afresh to the service of the Prince of Peace. It was then just two hundred years after the landing on Plymouth Rock. The second century in the history of the Pilgrim fathers and their descendants, was fitly closed by that period of

Christian activity and fruitfulness—was fitly crowned by that remarkable outpouring of the Spirit on the churches of New England. On the 22d of December, previous to the founding of our College, Daniel Webster delivered the oration on Forefathers' Day. It was a great occasion, worthy of the distinguished orator, and well improved by him in expatiating on the unforeseen and already far-reaching influence of that little Pilgrim band. But the 22d of December, 1870, the last anniversary preceding our semi-centennial, when Robert C. Winthrop addressed the New England Society, when the first quarter of the first millennium since the landing of the Pilgrims was consummated, was a still grander occasion, and registered a far wider and more rapid extension of their principles and spirit. The past year has been fitly celebrated as a year of jubilee by the sons of New England in every part of the world. And the College whose existence has been comprised between these two great epochs, whose birth-year synchronizes with the former, and its semi-centennial with the latter, has, we believe, borne its humble indeed, yet active and proper part in the propagation of the same principles, and rejoices to keep the same year of jubilee.

Charged, by the kindness of the Alumni, with the double duty of writing the history of the College, and of delivering an historical address at its semi-centennial celebration, my chief difficulty to-day lies in the selection of topics for this occasion. To avoid encroaching on the volume which is soon to be given to the press, and at the same time to restrict myself within the limits proper to this hour, I have thought it best, with the advice and concurrence also of your committee, to construct this address chiefly of "chips from the workshop" of the history. At the same time, I think you will see clearly enough that they are "chips from the old block," and so they may serve for "specimens" of the history as well.

As earth and man must conspire, under the guiding hand of Providence, to produce a race or a nation, so an institution that *lives,* is born of the age, the place, the people and the providence of God.   Such a College as ours clearly could never have come into existence in any other country than the United States, nor in any other of the United States than Massachusetts, nor anywhere else in Massachusetts but in the valley of the Connecticut, and old·Hampshire County.   The foundations for Amherst College were laid when this goodly valley was formed, and yonder beautiful river was sent winding like a silver thread through the vegetable mosaic of those matchless meadows—when those mountains were reared which compass it about like the mountains round about Jerusalem, and this consecrated eminence was elevated which was destined to become the Mount Zion, whither our tribes go up to their yearly festivals—nay, when the sandstone which underlies the valley, was made, with its broad and manifold·pages written all over with those ancient characters which our Hitchcock was to decipher, and our professors and students were to read and study through untold generations.   And some of the sources of its intellectual and moral life were provided when this changeful and stimulating climate was created, which ranges at different seasons through all the temperatures from the torrid to the frigid zone, and when the peculiar atmosphere and light of this valley were so attempered and so adjusted to this site, as to give us these magnificent sunsets, different indeed, but not inferior to those of Italy and Greece.   With still greater truth and emphasis the College may be said to have been the natural outgrowth of the peculiar intellectual, moral and religious characteristics of the people among whom it has taken root.   President Dwight, in his Travels through New England and New York, finds in the inhabitants of the towns and villages of the Connecticut valley a style of building and living, a style of thinking, speaking and acting quite their own, which he ascribes partly to their origin and early isolation from the other colonies, and partly to the soil, climate, surface and other physical features of the country. He gives them credit for industry and thrift, for general intelligence, virtue and piety, and for an equality of social condition and culture beyond the average, even of New England. The county of Hampshire was long ago recognized as the banner county in the number of its educated men, and the proportion of its church members. It is only the legitimate offspring of such a population, the natural and indigenous growth, as it were, of the soil, that we see when we behold Amherst College, Williston Seminary, Mount Holyoke Seminary, the Massachusetts Agricultural College, and the two Smith Colleges (already located and soon to be built at Northampton), springing up one after another, all in the same county, in a single half century, (like the Academy, the Lyceum, and those other immortal schools which sprung from the soil of Attica), and distinguishing this as the banner county of the State and the nation in the number and character of its educational institutions.

There was a project for establishing a College in Northampton, Hadley, or Hatfield, several years previous to the Revolution. A charter was issued by the Colonial Governor, Stephen Bernard, constituting Israel Billings and eleven others a corporation under the name of "The President and Fellows of Queen's College." The corporation held two or three meetings, and a beginning was perhaps made in the instruction of a few students. But the opposition of the friends of Harvard College arrested its progress, and the Revolution soon diverted the attention of the people to more exciting scenes. The first definite and public proposition for the establishment of a College at Amherst, so far as we can learn, was made in the Franklin

Association of Congregational ministers, assembled at the house
of Rev. Theophilus Packard in Shelburne, May 10, 1815, when, in
answer to a question proposed by Brother Packard, it was unanimously resolved by that body, that "in their opinion, knowledge
and virtue might be greatly subserved by a literary institution
situated in some central town of old Hampshire County," and
they were also "unanimously agreed that, all things considered,
the town of Amherst appeared to them the most eligible place
for locating it." This first associated action, it will be observed,
took place six years previous to the opening of Amherst College, and it took place, not in Hampshire, but Franklin County,
and not even in the Connecticut valley, but among the mountains almost half-way from Amherst to Williamstown. Mr.
Packard was a trustee of Williams College, and the ministers
of Franklin Association were among the best friends and patrons of that institution. Yet, rising above all personal attachments and local preferences, with a single eye to the best
method of promoting "knowledge and virtue," they unanimously
recommend the establishment of a College in the valley of the
Connecticut and in the center of Hampshire County.

The project for removing Williams College to some central
town in Hampshire County, preceded any efforts or plans for
founding Amherst College; it originated with the friends of
Williams, it received the votes of nine out of twelve of the
trustees of that institution, and was zealously prosecuted by
them as the best way of advancing its prosperity, and perhaps
the only means of perpetuating its existence, till, at length, the
Legislature of Massachusetts put an end to the project, by
refusing the permission which they asked for its removal.

Amherst Academy was the mother of Amherst College, its
founders were the founders of the College also, and the trustees
of the former were the trustees of the latter during those four

eventful years in which it was struggling to obtain a separate charter. This Academy was opened to receive students in December, 1814, and under the instruction of superior teachers, guided by enlightened trustees, and fostered by a sympathizing community, it rose immediately to the first rank among the academies of the State, and continued for many years to exert a leading educational and Christian influence. Not content with this, the trustees, at the suggestion of "Rufus Graves, Esq.," made an effort in the fall of 1817 to "increase the usefulness of the Academy" by raising a fund for the endowment of a Professorship of Languages in it, and the gratuitous education of young men for the Christian ministry. But even the indefatigable Colonel Graves found it impossible to raise money for this object. Nothing daunted by this failure, the trustees only enlarged their plan, struck for a College instead of an Academy, and set out to raise a charity fund, not of ten thousand, but of fifty thousand dollars. At their meeting on the 18th of August, 1818, they unanimously accepted as the basis of such an institution, the constitution and by-laws reported by Colonel Graves, under which that charity fund was raised, and has ever since been administered, which has proved, indeed, the sheet-anchor of Amherst College. On the 29th day of September, 1818, a convention of thirty-six clergymen and thirty-two laymen, representing thirty-seven towns and forty parishes in Hampshire, Hampden and Franklin Counties, and the western section of Worcester County, met in Amherst at the call of the trustees, and after much animated discussion, especially touching the location, by a very large majority sanctioned their plan and proceedings. One speech is said to have exerted a controlling influence in securing this result. It was the maiden speech of George Grennell, secretary of the convention, afterwards for ten years member of Congress, and more than twenty years trustee of Amherst College.

The fifty thousand dollars charity fund was raised in less than a single year.   After considerable delay in efforts to unite Williams College and the Institution at Amherst, the first building, the old South College, was commenced.   The corner-stone was laid August 9, 1820, an address being de-livered on the occasion by Noah Webster, and a characteristic sermon, entitled "A Plea for a Miserable World," by Rev. Dan-iel A. Clark, then pastor of the First Church and Society in Am-herst.   The walls went up and the roof was ready for shingling in ninety days.   Before the next autumn, the interior was fin-ished and a part of the rooms furnished for the reception of students; and on the 18th of September, 1821, the College was opened with the ceremonies of dedication and inauguration, as already stated, and the examination of students for the several classes.   Thus old Massachusetts, who before held Harvard College in her right hand, and Williams in her left, now had a College near her geographical heart; and near it was also to the hearts of her orthodox, evangelical, Christian people.   Animated by the spirit of the revivals that were then prevailing, and the missions which they were then organizing, inspired by a jealous love for the truth which, as they believed, was then assailed at a vital point, and by an earnest desire for the salvation of perish-ing men, they felt deeply the need of a College more advantage-ously situated than Williams, to fill the place which Harvard had lost in their confidence and affections, to be the radiating point of a truly Christian education and influence, and espe-cially to educate pastors for their churches, ministers for the new settlements, and missionaries for the great and growing field both at home and in foreign lands.   Such were the motives that moved the ministers of Franklin Association and others of like character in Hampshire, Hampden and Worcester Counties —Packard and Taylor, and Porter and Crosby, and Fiske and

Snell, and Vaill and Keep—to pray and labor for the establishment of Amherst College. Such were the considerations which, when presented by these ministers, and more directly by Colonel Graves and other agents, stirred up intelligent Christian laymen in every part of Massachusetts, irrespective of local preferences, to give so promptly and liberally to the charity fund.

And this, I verily believe, was the strongest motive which impelled the Christian men and women of Amherst to give so much of their time and toil and money—the product of their farms, the growth of their forests, the labor of their hands, and contributions of every kind to the erection of the College buildings. For the people of Amherst were, after all, the real founders of Amherst College. They were by far the largest and most liberal contributors to the charity fund. And such a foundation was then a new and unprecedented, a bold and vast undertaking. To raise fifty thousand dollars then for such a purpose, was a more difficult and ·daring enterprise than it would be now to raise half a million. They also took upon themselves the chief burden of putting up the first edifice. They gave the land, and prepared the site, and laid the foundations and furnished the materials, and put their hands in every possible way to the work. They paid and fed the masons and 'carpenters—the first men in Amherst tended them, if necessary, in person, and their wives and daughters ministered to them with their own hands. They may almost be said to have camped on the ground, and considering the opposition which they encountered, to have "labored with the sword in one hand, and the implement of the builder in the other, for the people had a mind to work; and none of them put off their clothes, saving that every one put them off for washing," and not a few of them might also have said: we have mortgaged our lands, vineyards and houses, that the work might go forward without

interruption to its accomplishment.   In short, if the scene ever
had any precedent or parallel, it was in the rebuilding of the
walls of Jerusalem by the Jews, as recorded in the Book of Ne-
hemiah — a passage, by the way, which our good President
Humphrey used to read in the chapel at evening prayers, whenever the burden of building the College grew very heavy, or
there was a fresh outbreak of opposition from " Geshem, Tobiah
and Sanballat."   And here let me bear this public testimony
to the good people of Amherst, that from the first breaking
of the ground on College Hill, nay, from the first opening
of the subscription, to this day, there has never been an emergency in the history of the College, in which they have not been
the first to put their shoulders to the wheel, and the last to
withdraw from bearing the heavy burden.

The time would fail me to mention even the names of the
noble, heroic Christian men and women of Amherst, who thus
labored in laying the foundations of this Institution.   Yet there
are a few to whom universal suffrage would assign the pre-emi-
nence, and to whose character and services justice demands
that we pay a passing tribute on this occasion.   The name
of one of these springs to our lips at the bare mention of the
charity fund ; at the very thought of it we see him, tall, slen-
der, plainly clad, his head sprinkled already with the frosts of
years, leaving but a scanty provision for his wife and children,
setting out on his pilgrimage of begging, not for himself, not
even for the College or the Church, but "for the Lord," going
from house to house in Amherst, till, at length, his old horse refused to be driven past any door, and then extending his
circuits from town to town, not only through that famous "circle of fifty miles around, of which Amherst was the center," but
in almost every county of the old Bay State.   Born in Sunderland in 1758, he was already more than sixty years of age.   But

he was one of those men who never grow old. A graduate of Dartmouth in the class of 1791, in 1812 a lecturer on chemistry in the College where he was educated, as he afterward was for a short time in the Academy and in the College of which he helped to lay the foundations, a bold but not very successful experimenter in fancy farming in Leverett, in building a tide-mill in Boston, and in selling patent milking machines in Franklin County, at length taking up his residence in the second story of the Academy building, he devoted several years of his life to the scarcely less doubtful, though finally successful, experiment of founding and building up Amherst College. He wrote the constitution and by-laws of the charity fund. He did more than any one else toward raising the money. He was the first Secretary of the Board of Trustees, and the first lecturer on chemistry, in a private room then used for lectures and recitations in the old South College. He lived on for several years after he had done his work here, and died in 1846 at Portsmouth, Ohio, at the age of four score years and six. Ardent almost to enthusiasm, more remarkable for zeal than for prudence, enterprising and versatile, a colonel in the militia, an officer in the church, a man of prayer, full of faith and of the Holy Ghost, a loving and beloved disciple who leaned on the bosom of his Lord, and took counsel with Him first of all in every emergency, Rufus Graves, Esq., as Mr. Webster always calls him, Colonel Graves, as he is known to the community, was fitted by nature, education and grace to be beyond any other man a pioneer in the enterprise of raising money, and being also without business, and devoting his whole time for so many years to the work, to him by common consent is generally assigned the first place among the founders of Amherst College.

Without the indefatigable agency and impulsive power of

some such man as Colonel Graves, it is probable that Amherst College would never have come into existence. But it is quite çertain that the College never could have been founded wholly by such men as he. A vessel must not only have sails but ballast, before it can safely launch out into the broad ocean. Our ubiquitous and persistent agent abroad had a no less unwearied and devoted coadjutor at home, who possessed property, influence, and some traits of character in which the former was deficient. A native of Amherst, an alumnus of Dartmouth, where, though the youngest member, he was the second scholar in his class, a student of law in the office of Judge Strong, one of the ablest members of the bar of Hampshire County, who might have had a seat on the bench if he had not chosen to turn aside and engage in business, a deacon in the church from the age of twenty-one, town clerk for fourteen years, a member at different times of both branches of the Legislature, Samuel Fowler Dickinson, Esq., devoted wisdom and experience, professional influence and personal service, time, toil and money without stint, to the founding and building up, first of Amherst Academy and then of Amherst College, till he sacrificed his profession, his business, and at length his property, to these great educational and public interests. The enlargement of the plan from a mere professorship in the Academy to the founding of a College, is believed to have originated with him ; it certainly received from him the most intelligent advocacy and the most effective support. It is known that the work on the College buildings would have stopped many times for want of means, if he had not obtained money from the bank on his personal credit, and also turned in his own teams and men, and sometimes taken hold of the work with his own hands. It is one of those sad events, incident to the imperfection of all human enterprises, that this large-minded, large-hearted, public-spirited, self-sacrificing man, who had done so much for the College and the public, felt at length that his services were not appreciated, and went away, with inextinguishable zeal and benevolence, to render similar services in his old age to Lane Seminary and Western Reserve College. He died at Hudson, Ohio, in 1838, at the age of 62. But his remains rest in yonder cemetery, in full view of the beloved College of which history will justly recognize him as one of the principal founders ; and if his spirit is permitted to revisit the scene of his earthly cares and toils, and to participate with us in these jubilee services, with what supreme satisfaction, wonder and joy must he look upon the unimagined results of his labors and sacrifices !

With Colonel Graves and Esquire Dickinson was associated a third co-worker, who, in character and condition, was a sort of medium between them. The son of a Judge of the Supreme Court of Massachusetts, whose ancestral dwelling is one of the celebrities of Amherst, a lawyer by education and profession, not less self-sacrificing and public-spirited than Esquire Dickinson, scarcely less enthusiastic and visionary than Colonel Graves, Hezekiah Wright Strong was not behind either in devotion to the public good. Indeed, he was one of those men who are always in advance of their neighbors and their age, and always trying experiments, of which others sooner or later reap the chief benefits. To his almost quixotic enterprise, Amherst was indebted for its first ice-house, its first bathing-house, and (queer enough, but not more queer than characteristic,) the first importation of a wagon-load of Congress water! which, in a small country town, of course, did not turn out a brilliant speculation. To his zeal and personal agency, Amherst Academy largely owed its existence. Claiming to be the father of the Academy, he sometimes playfully remarked that he was thus the grandfather of the College. He also claimed the credit of having selected the site for the first College edifice, and set the first stake on the grounds. Which of these three men originated the idea of voluntary contributions of labor and materials for the first building, or whether it sprang up simultaneously in the minds of many, and which made the greatest sacrifices in the early establishment of the College, are questions which have been discussed, but need not be answered. They all did what they could, and all deserve honorable remembrance together as "the first three" among the Amherst founders.

There was a fourth who contributed more than either of the three to give character and reputation to the new enterprise, perhaps also to guide and guard the incipient measures. Noah Webster came to Amherst in 1812, attracted at once by the quiet beauty of the place and the economy of living here. He had already published his American Spelling-Book, and the entire support of his family during his ten years' residence in Amherst and his twenty years' labor on the American Dictionary, was derived from the profits of this work, at a copyright of less than one cent on a copy. Scholar and student as he was, Dr. Webster identified himself with the people among whom he dwelt, was often moderator in town meetings and chairman of church committees, represented the town three years in the General Court, and received the votes of his townsmen as a candidate for Congress, contributed much, with the help of his accomplished wife and daughters, to the elevation and refinement of society, and lent all his influence to the planting and growth of the Academy and the College, both of which originated while he was a resident of Amherst. He was Vice-President of the Board of Trustees till Dr. Parsons resigned the presidency at the laying of the corner-stone of the first College edifice, and President of the Board thereafter till, at the opening of the College, he resigned to make room for the election of President Moore to that office. Soon after this he removed to New Haven. This distinguished philologist and educator, whose spelling-book has done more to form the character of the masses than any other book in the English language except the Bible, and whose dictionary is more than any other the standard of that language wherever it is spoken, was, as his addresses show, a humble and earnest Christian, in full sympathy with the orthodox creed and missionary spirit of the other founders; and we may well be proud to associate his name with the early history of our College.

Nathaniel Smith of Sunderland was the largest pecuniary benefactor of the College, under the first two Presidents. Indeed, this successful banker, this wise counselor, this devoted friend of education, religion, missions and every good cause, was more than any other man the Samuel Williston of Amherst in those early days; and it is difficult .to see how the College could have been established or sustained through many a trying emergency, without his (for the time) princely liberality. He had the honor of being omitted, nay, excluded (that is not too strong a word,) *excluded* from the Corporation by the Legislature which gave the charter, and restored to the position, which, according to every rule of justice and right, belonged to him, by the Legislature three years later. How much President Humphrey leaned upon this tall, stalwart man, who was one of Nature's noblemen, may be seen from the sermon, entitled "The Good Arimathean," which he preached at his funeral.

We would gladly linger at these fountains. Two other names must receive a passing mention—Rev. Dr. David Parsons, the first President of the Board, whose preaching, during a pastorate of forty years, did so much to educate the people of

Amherst and prepare them for the arduous enterprise of founding a Christian College, and Rev. Daniel A. Clark, his successor
in the pastoral office, whose powerful sermons not only moved
the first generation of students while they were here, but became
the model after which many of them preached the Gospel
in subsequent years.   But we must hasten on to the more immediate actors.

The first President was remarkably fitted for the work which
he was providentially raised up to accomplish.   Born in Palmer,
Mass., and brought up in Wilmington, Vt., he learned by early
experience to sympathize with the sons of farmers and of the
laboring classes.   After graduating at Dartmouth, teaching a
short time in the Academy at Londonderry, N. H., and studying theology with Dr. Backus, in Somers, Ct., he was eleven
years pastor of the church in Leicester, Mass., four years Professor of Languages in Dartmouth College, and six years President of Williams.   Entire success. in each of these spheres
of duty qualified him for and elevated him to the next, and he
brought to the presidency at Amherst the wisdom and experience which he had accumulated in them all.   As a man,
President Moore was remarkably winning and attractive.   He
weighed over two hundred pounds, yet without any appearance
of obesity.   A gentleman of the old school, retaining the use
of short breeches and long hose, which were particularly becoming to his person, and exhibiting in his manner a rare union
of suavity with dignity, he won his way immediately to the
hearts of all his pupils, while at the same time he invariably
commanded their profound respect and obedience.   None of us
can look upon his portrait, which hangs in our library, without
being reminded of the language of Tacitus in his Life of Agri-
cola: "decentior quam sublimior fuit; nihil metus in vultu,
gratia oris supererat; bonum virum facile crederes, magnum

libenter." While he entered most cordially into the religious views and plans of the founders and the characteristic spirit of "the Collegiate Institution at Amherst," he insisted, as a condition to his acceptance of the presidency, that "the classical education of the students should be thorough," and "the course of study should not be inferior to that in the Colleges in New England." At the same time he was in advance of the age in his appreciation of the modern physical sciences, and thus early gave to individual students, if not to the College, something of that bent by which it has ever since been distinguished. In addition to his appropriate duties as President, and as Chairman of the Board of Trustees, Doctor Moore heard all the recitations of the Senior class, and in part those of the Sophomore. A precious revival of religion in the spring term of his second year, while it gladdened his heart beyond measure, as it did also those of the friends of the infant seminary, added greatly to his labors and responsibilities. At the same time he was soliciting money to meet the pecuniary necessities of the Institution, and pressing its claims for a charter upon a reluctant, and to a great extent, hostile Legislature. The failure of the second application to the General Court at its spring session, superadded to such overwhelming labors, cares and anxieties, was too much for him to bear. An attack of acute disease, a few days after his return from Boston, soon overpowered his exhausted system, and he died on Monday, the 30th of June, 1823, in the fifty-third year of his age. Every student felt that he had lost a father. To many, in and out of the College, the death of its President, under such circumstances, seemed to be a death-blow to the Institution. The Senior class asked to be excused from performing their parts at the ensuing Commencement, and seeing no reasonable prospect of ever being able to obtain a diploma here, they began to look about for other places of graduation. But courage revived, faith and hope triumphed, and so far from dying, the infant seminary soon entered on a new and higher stage of its existence.

The Faculty, as first organized under President Moore, consisted of two Professors and two Tutors. The Professor of Mathematics and Natural Philosophy, Rev. Gamaliel S. Olds, a graduate of Williams College, was a man of strong mind, a good classical scholar, and master of the whole field of mathematics. But there was in him an element of over-sensitiveness, not to say of personal ambition and insubordination, which had already cut short his connection with two or three other Colleges, and his relation to Amherst College ceased with the organization of the Faculty anew under the charter in 1825. The Professor of Greek and Latin, Mr. Joseph Estabrook, an alumnus of Dartmouth, won an enviable reputation as Principal of Amherst Academy during the three years which preceded the opening of the College, but, if we may judge from the silence of the letters of alumni, does not seem to have made a very strong impression on the College students. Being subject to a bronchial affection, he resigned his professorship in 1824, and was afterward President for thirteen years of the University of East Tennessee. Lucius Field, a graduate of Williams, was the first Tutor. He was also the first superintendent of the first Sabbath-school in Amherst. Tutor Burt, a graduate of Union, is mentioned with respect in the letters of early alumni, is still spoken of in town as the instrument of the conversion of every member of his class in the Sabbath-school, and is gratefully remembered by many whom he fitted for College in Belchertown, Monson, Hadley, and Ithica, New York. The students of those early days possessed in large measure the same spirit which animated the founders of the College. Otherwise they never would have come here for their education. Even now I can not help wondering that they did come. They could not go far in any direction without meeting those who would fain dissuade them from coming, by every argument which wit and wisdom could devise, especially by that argument which it is most difficult for young men to withstand, ridicule and sarcasm. A venerable clergyman met one of these early students when he was a member of the academy, and, pointing to the first edifice (then in process of erection), said, "They are putting up that building only to be a habitation for the moles and the bats." An honored teacher in a neighboring academy, said to the same young man about the same time: "When Amherst College is started, I suppose they will grind out ministers as fast as they do corn at the grist-mill." That young man entered Amherst College, notwithstanding, and went through that grist-mill, and came out as good a minister as any church need ever desire, and I believe he is here to-day to rejoice in results which have falsified all such sinister prophecies, and turned enemies to friends.

These early students were conscious that their literary and scientific advantages were not of the highest order. But they made the best use of all they had. Most of them came here for no other purpose but to gain knowledge and discipline, that they might be useful. The largest part of them were Christian young men, who studied with the highest and holiest motives. And they found no small compensation for their inferior advantages in their freedom from distracting scenes. They had neither concerts nor lectures, cattle shows nor Jim Crows to tempt them from their lessons. Nor did they study in the dazzle and glare of universal publicity, with the eyes of the world staring at them, and lines of magnetic communication connecting their brain and nervous system with the ends of the earth. And they made good scholars—great and good men.

In proof of this we have only to mention the names of David
O. Allen, Elijah Paine, Bela B. Edwards, George Shepard, John
Taylor Jones, Henry W. Strong, Elijah C. Bridgman, and Arte-
mas Bullard, among the illustrious dead (to say nothing of the'
distinguished living) who began, at least, and some of them finished their course under President Moore.   They loved their
College, and almost worshiped their President.   Their relations
to the good people of the town were even more intimate and
endearing than those of students now-a-days; perhaps some of
the young men who hear me will hardly believe this.   They
worshiped with them in the church, sung with them in the
choir, taught in their Sabbath and day schools, and not only the
school-master, but the singing-master and leader of the choir
sometimes "boarded round" for a part of his pay.   And in
these earliest times the precedent was established of entering
into still more endearing and enduring relations.   Whether
"Confidence Lot" and "Lovers' Gròve" received their significant names at this time, or at a still earlier period, is a question
in antiquities which I have not been able to solve.   Certain
it is—judging from the letters of alumni which read amazingly
like love-letters—certain it is that those were halcyon days.   It
was the romantic if not also the heroic age of our College.
Perhaps some of my hearers will suspect that it was the mythi-
cal age in our history.

The second President introduces us to what our Professor of
Ecclesiastical History, in a speech at one of our alumni meetings, called the mediæval period.   He was not less admirably
fitted than his predecessor to meet the emergencies of the time
and the place, and to accomplish the work which now needed
to be done for the College.   The Institution was still an infant
of less than two years old when it was bereaved of its first
President.   It had no charter.   Its hold on life was precarious.

Two plain and rude dormitories constituted the homestead, and the charity fund, much of which as yet existed only on paper, was its sole inheritance. The $30,000 subscription was completed just before the death of President Moore. But it was payable in five annual instalments, and at every stage of its collection was more than balanced by debts. There was no church organization, no chapel for morning and evening prayers or the worship of the Sabbath. Such a thing as an observatory, a cabinet or a library building had never even been thought of. A handful of books, chiefly contributed by the neighboring ministers, went by the name of a library; a few pieces of second-hand apparatus, given by friends or picked up where they could be bought the cheapest, then represented all our present collections; a few extemporized benches, arranged around a rude, extemporized desk, served for chapel, lecture-room and place of general convocation, and all these were crowded together in one end of the fourth story of the new North College. In short, it was the "Collegiate Institution of Amherst." AMHERST COLLEGE was yet to be created. This was the work which devolved on Dr. Humphrey. And with the blessing of God he accomplished it.

The son of a Connecticut farmer in humble circumstances, he worked out on a farm every summer, and, after his own brief school-boy days were ended, taught school every winter till he was twenty-five. After only six months of uninterrupted study, during which he made all his preparation in Greek and much of his preparation in Latin and mathematics, he entered the Junior class of Yale College, where he "paid all the expenses of his own education, except that some of his clothes were furnished by his mother;" and yet he received an oration for his graduating appointment at Commencement. Thus was he fitted to preside over a College so many of whose students were to go through a similar experience. Thus, also, he acquired the stalwart frame and robust health of body, mind and heart which enabled him to sustain the heavy burden, as well as the firm self-reliance, the strong common sense, the quick faculty of observation, the knowledge of men and things, and the sympathy with the masses, which were among the main secrets of his strength. A pastorate of ten years in Fairfield, Conn., and of six years in Pittsfield, Mass., during which, besides being the wise, faithful, successful, honored and beloved shepherd of his own flock, he was a leader in revivals, reformations, missions and every other form of public charity and benevolence, qualified him to be the President of a College so large a proportion of whose graduates in his day were to be ministers, and at the same time rooted him in the confidence and affections of the churches, whose sympathy and support were to be his chief reliance in laying broader and deeper the foundations of the Institution.

President Humphrey accepted the office, against the remonstrances of his people and his personal inclination, from an imperative sense of duty, and came to Amherst to assume its responsibilities with fear and anxiety. But his inaugural address was like the sound of a trumpet, inspiring the founders of the College with new courage, rallying the hesitating to its support, enlisting the sympathy of the friends of learning wedded to religion, and attracting students from afar. Hardly had he commenced the work of government and instruction before he was summoned to his first great battle—that of the Charter. We have not time to tell the story; nor need we. It has been often told. It was not so much a battle as a war. Sectional prejudices, local envy and jealousy, rival educational interests, hatred of orthodoxy, and hostility to evangelical religion, were all arrayed against the College. Twice already had its friends been defeated, nay, routed in the unequal conflict. The first President had just fallen in the midst of the fight. The second, like his predecessor, had not only to lead the forces, but to fight with one hand, and, at the same time, build with the other. But he was fully equal to the crisis. His appeals to the people, through the press, were clear, cogent, unanswerable. His speech before the joint committee of the two Houses, in the winter of 1824, was pronounced by candid and competent judges the ablest that was made in Boston during that session of the Legislature. Twice more were they beaten, but each time by a smaller majority. One more such gain would assure a victory. As a last resource of strategy, the enemies of the College moved a committee of investigation, and carried their point. But they soon wished they had not. The committee visited Amherst, searched everything to the bottom, but soon came to the conclusion that they were only collecting money, and making capital for the College; they therefore went back, and, as a matter of policy, recommended the granting of a charter, and their recommendation received the sanction of both branches of the Legislature. Thus, after a delay of three years and a half from the opening, and more than two years from the time of the first petition, the Institution obtained a charter, and Amherst was admitted to a name as well as a place among the colleges of Massachusetts. The charter was signed by Lieutenant-Governor Marcus Morton, then acting Governor in place of William T. Eustis, who had deceased a short time previous. Governor Eustis and Lieutenant-Governor Morton were the candidates of the Democratic party, elected by Federalist votes cast by friends of Amherst College, to whom party ties were less sacred than justice, learning and religion. The rival candidate for the gubernatorial office met Governor Eustis shortly after his election, and knowing how the political scales had been turned, said to him, "I understand your excellency is becoming orthodox." "I am not so sure of that," replied the Governor elect, "but at any rate, I believe in the doctrine of election." The charter dates from the 21st of February, 1825, and the seal of the College represents the sun and an open Bible illuminating the globe, while underneath is written the motto: "Terras irradient." God speed the fulfillment of the prophecy.

Meanwhile, the College Church had been organized, and a separate service instituted for worship on the Sabbath. The College Chapel was dedicated in February, 1827, and in 1828, the new North College was erected. Then followed the second great battle, which was more protracted and fierce than the first. The application to the Legislature for pecuniary aid met with more violent opposition, and called forth more bitter vituperation, than the petition for a charter. After five years of delay and suspense, of postponement and evasion, during which four successive committees had reported in favor of the College, the question was at length brought to a decisive issue, and the application was rejected, or which was the same thing, indefinitely postponed by a large majority. But the defeat was worth more than a victory. The money which the committees proposed, but the Legislature refused to grant, was raised by private subscription. And what neither officers nor students, funds nor friends, could have done for the College, was accomplished for it by the intemperate zeal of its enemies. In less than five years after it was chartered, it numbered more than two hundred students, and at the end of ten years, two hundred and fifty, thus ranking in this respect second only to Yale.

The able and excellent Faculty whom President Humphrey gathered about him, contributed their full share to this result. The Faculty of Amherst College, as it appears on the catalogue of 1825, and as it was first fully organized under the charter, consisted of Rev Heman Humphrey, Rev. Edward Hitchcock, Rev. Nathan W. Fiske, Rev. Solomon Peck, Samuel M. Worcester, Jacob Abbot, and Ebenezer S. Snell. Of these seven persons, four have finished their course, and may, therefore, be spoken of without flattery or prejudice. And what one of them can ever be forgotten or dissevered from the history of Amherst College? Humphrey, wise, strong, unselfish, magnanimous, the very impersonation of robust common sense, perfect sincerity, stainless honor and unswerving Christian principle—Hitchcock, genius, science and enthusiasm sanctified and inspired by religion—Fiske, the accurate scholar, the acute metaphysician, the powerful preacher, whom God *did*, and man did *not*, make a Doctor of Divinity—and Worcester, with his varied reading and unbounded memory and inexhaustible affluence of diction, *made* apparently for a professor of rhetoric and oratory, yet so fond of the work of the ministry that he relinquished his professorship for the pastoral office—each exactly fitted for his place, and all uniting as one man in unwearied labors for the prosperity of the College and the advancement of Christian education. Of the six others who came into the Faculty at different times under the presidency of Dr. Humphrey, one only has departed this life—the lamented Hovey, of whom it may be confidently said, that if his bodily health and strength had equaled his talents, virtues and accomplishments, his would have been one of the most honored and beloved names in the history of Amherst College. Of the survivors, only two are still connected with the Faculty. One of us has been a professor forty-two years, the other thirty-five, long enough already to be counted among the antiquities of the College. If we should continue much longer, we shall probably be classed with the fossils of the antediluvian age. The rest—Professors Abbott and Peck of the original Faculty, and Professors Clark,

7

Condit, Fowler and Warner who came in later—live to adorn
other stations, and to show how skillful Amherst has been in
finding and forming professors for theological seminaries—how
excellent a school the Faculty of Amherst has been for training
authors, scholars, secretaries, and in the original and proper
sense of the term, doctors of divinity.   Connected with the
College but a few years at most, they of course contributed less
to form the character of the Institution.   But they added lustre
to the administration of President Humphrey, made their mark
on at least two or three classes, and grateful memories of their
life and teaching here are rooted in the hearts of not a few who
are gathered within these walls to-day.

The Tutors, too—those afflicted and persecuted souls who,
through much tribulation, at length enter into rest and inherit
the promises—Bela B. Edwards, Joseph S. Clark, William P.
Paine, Story Hebard, Ezekiel Russell, H. B. Hackett, Justin
Perkins, W. S. Tyler, Timothy Dwight, Edward P. Humphrey,
Ebenezer Burgess, Elbridge Bradbury, Thatcher Thayer, Wel-
lington H. Tyler, Charles Clapp, S. Boltwood Ingram, Calvin
E. Park, Amos Bullard, George C. Partridge, C. B. Adams,
Thomas P. Field, Clinton Clark, John Humphrey, William A.
Peabody, J. G. D. Stearns, Roswell D. Hitchcock, Charles E.
Washburn, Thomas S. Miller, George B. Jewett, H. M. Spof-
ford, Rowland Ayres—what hallowed names are these in the
memory of some of our hearts—what places of honor do many
of them now hold in literature, science, theology and religion—
and how much higher do many of them (too many, alas! for us
and our dear mother's joy, for almost half of them have received their crown,) how much higher do many of them shine
among those that have turned many to righteousness!

As these were not only tutors but alumni, they may serve
also as specimens of the men and the scholars that were edu-

cated here, even in this mediæval period of our history. And I should call up names scarcely less honored, memories no less sacred at least to classmates and friends, should I venture to speak of others, not tutors, one or more in every class, who, some very early, and all too early, have finished the work of life —A. W. McClure, Reuben Tinker, Isaac Bliss, Henry Lyman, James L. Merrick, Moody Harrington, James Humphrey, Simeon Shurtleff, Hosea D. Humphrey, Alonzo Gray, Eli Thurston, William B. Homer, Alexander Montgomery, Johnathan B. Marshall, James H. Bancroft, Joel E. Everett, Henry M. Bridgman, R. S. Storrs Dickinson, and others still, living as well as dead, quite too numerous to mention.

A member of the class that graduated just at the close of the first decade of years, in a letter, has characterized that decade as the age of experiments. It was then that the experiment of the parallel course, substituting the physical sciences and the modern languages for the ancient classics, was tried and failed, vanishing when the class with which it was inaugurated, had scarcely yet finished their course, and leaving "not a rack behind," except the wisdom to those who tried it, and the warning to others, which were contained in the experience. Then, too, the students, with the consent of the Faculty, were organized into a body politic, with legislative and judiciary departments, and tried the experiment of self-government in internal affairs and social relations, till, after some useful and many amusing experiences, that class of students described in the two lines of Hudibras :—

> " For none e'er felt the halter draw,
> With good opinion of the law,"

finding it a little too much of an "imperium in imperio," rose in rebellion and overthrew the government. The old gymnasium—the gymnasium in the grove, with its swings, parallel bars, wooden horses and stadia for running and jumping—originated at this time; and many will perhaps agree with our Anglo-Saxon Professor, of the class of '45, that the old grove as we then used it, was better than the biggest stone gymnasium.

The decade which began with the College charter, ending of course with 1835, was the period of rapid growth and enlargement. We have already spoken of the rapid increase of students. The two Professors and two Tutors that Dr. Humphrey found when he first came here, grew under his administration into a Faculty of ten or twelve, of whom five or six were regular Professors, four were Tutors, and the rest were special instructors, or occasional lecturers, the auxiliaries, ξένοι as the old Greeks would call them, not much to be depended on, yet some of them, as Dr. Post and Hon. William B. Calhoun, gave us some very excellent lectures. At the same time, valuable additions were made by purchases in ·Europe to the library, philosophical apparatus and other material of education to correspond with the growing number of students. This same decade was the golden age of the literary societies when they had not yet had their life-blood sucked out of them by a swarm of Greek letter fraternities—when the Social Union, although she entered the course only in Sophomore year, as it were, (do my hearers understand the figure?) and though she always had the credit of being a little sophomorical in her relations to the government, waked up the Alexandrian and Athenian Societies to a generous rivalry, the fruit of which was seen in full meetings and eloquent debates, as well as growing libraries, and when at the invitation of the literary societies every Commencement, such orators as Gov. Everett of Massachusetts and Gov. McDowell of Virginia pronounced those model orations which stirred the young men to a noble emulation as Thucydides was stirred by the rehearsals of Herodotus at the Olympic games—as the youthful Themistocles was excited when he—

—" rustling heard in every breeze
The laurels of Miltiades."

The Antivenenian Society also came into existence at this time, and began that long and still lengthening roll of honor which has received the signatures of so large a proportion of the officers and students ever since, which President Hitchcock, then Professor, used to unroll with so much satisfaction before the wondering eyes of the Freshmen, and which he esteemed as almost a second charter of the rights, liberties and privileges of Amherst College.

We are indebted to John Tappan of Boston for the existence of this society, and vice versa, we are in part indebted to this society for the continued favor and life-long friendship of that enlightened Christian philanthropist, who began his benefactions to the College at a time of great prosperity, and never withdrew them in the darkest hour of adversity, and whose repeated donations to the library enlarged the minds and refreshed the spirits of officers and students, at seasons when they were almost starving for intellectual nourishment.

It was under the administration of President Humphrey that revivals of religion, of which there had been only one before his accession, were of such frequent and regular occurrence, were so labored for every year, and looked for at least once in four years, that it became a sort of law that no class had graduated, and none must be allowed to graduate without enjoying at least one such feast of ingathering. Beginning with 1827 and ending with 1831, there were three revivals in five years, and as the fruit of them, the ungodly and profane became pure in their hearts and lips and lives, the indolent and dissipated were made scholars, some who seemed to have as little intellect as scholar-

ship, developed surprising talents, and others whose genius and
wit made them the recognized leaders of their classes, although
they were devoid of religious principle, received a new direction, and went out to exert a commanding Christian influence
in the church and in the state, at home and in foreign lands.

In short, the administration of President Humphrey, scarcely
less than that of his predecessor, was our book of Genesis, in
which many of our organizations, usages and characteristic
traits had their origin, and at the same time our Exodus when
we went up out of Egypt, obtained our charter and our laws,
among the rest those College laws which were then as minute
and specific, and, in the opinion of some students, as mysterious
and severe as the laws of Moses that were given to the Israel-
ites in the wilderness.   It was the period when precedents were
established, principles settled, habits formed, and that character
fixed which our College still retains, and doubtless will retain
more or less in all coming time—when, in the favorite language
of the President, whom we so much honored, our Zion not only
"lengthened her cords and strengthened her stakes," but laid
the foundations, to some extent the literary, but still more the
moral and religious " foundations for many generations."

But the spring-tide of prosperity which ran so high for many
years, was at length naturally and inevitably followed by an
ebb.   The causes which had produced so unprecedented a
growth, and a growth, it must be confessed, which was not altogether natural and healthy, ceased to operate, or lost in a
measure their pristine power.   The fervor of a first love and
zeal for orthodoxy and evangelical piety had somewhat cooled.
The passion for missions and the education of ministers was
perhaps abated.   Revivals became less frequent in the churches.
The number of students now began to diminish.   Meanwhile
the debt, unavoidably contracted for the erection of buildings

in the day of prosperity, and annually increased by the current expenses and the payment of interest, was rapidly accumulating Subscriptions were again resorted to, and through the strenuous and persevering exertions of our accomplished agent, Rev. Mr. Vaill, a considerable sum was raised—nominally a hundred thousand dollars. But it is an inherent infelicity of subscriptions in small sums from all classes of individuals, that while there is the strongest temptation to swell the amount on paper and in the public estimation, an immense percentage is always lost in the collection. The earlier subscriptions to the funds of the College were worth more to it than the same amount would have been, if given in large donations or granted by the Legislature ; for every subscriber was a friend and patron, having an investment in the Institution. But the people grew weary at length of perpetual solicitations, and then the process made more enemies than friends. The poverty and opposition theory in the college, like the persecution theory in the church, is very true and very good within certain limits. But beyond those limits it is the reverse of the truth. The blood of the martyrs is the seed of the church. But the massacre of St. Bartholomew drowned and almost extinguished the French Protestants. Poverty and opposition nourished and strengthened Amherst College for the first fifteen years, but in the next ten years the same causes brought it to the verge of ruin. The debt was not canceled. The numbers continued to decrease. Disaffection sprung up in some of the classes, went forth with the graduates, and spread through the community. Embarrassments of every kind, nearly all, however, more or less connected with pecuniary difficulties, thickened and pressed harder and heavier upon the College, till the Trustees, who, by the blessing of God, had seen the Institution carried safely through its early trials, began seriously to fear that they might live to see it desolate and forsaken.

Professor Hitchcock was just the man for this emergency. Identified with the College in almost its entire previous history, idolized by the students and trusted by the alumni, enjoying the confidence of the Christian community, known personally by his geological explorations in every town of the State, and honored as a man of science by the savants of Europe as well as throughout his own country, his personal reputation and his wise policy, (I repeat it, and I mean just what I say,) *his personal reputation and his wise policy* SAVED THE COLLEGE. The first thing was to stop the leak that threatened to sink the ship, and at the same time to cease from asking pecuniary aid of the public, already weary of such solicitations. At his suggestion, with the consent of the Trustees, the President and Professors resolved to stay, at all events, the further increase of the debt by farming the revenues themselves, and receiving for their support the net income, however much it might fall below their regular salaries and the necessary expenses. This self-denying effort awakened public sympathy, and a series of measures was commenced, which, during the ten years of Doctor Hitchcock's presidency, extinguished the debt, added an astronomical observatory, a library, and two cabinets of natural history to the public buildings, secured the permanent endowment of four professorships, together with valuable funds for the purchase of books and immense scientific collections, and doubled the number of under-graduates.

We have no time for the details, scarcely even for an allusion to our benefactors. One towers far above the rest, and indeed above all the pecuniary benefactors of the College, in the number, variety and timeliness of his gifts, and in the relative value, though he is exceeded by one in the absolute sum of his donations. It is quite unnecessary to mention the name of Samuel Williston, who, if he did not save the College from extinction,

established it for the first time on a solid and enduring foundation. To him Cicero's claim for everlasting remembrance as
the preserver and second founder of Rome, applies in all the
cogency of the argument, in all the beauty and significance of
the language: "Si non minus nobis jucundi atque illustres
sunt ii dies quibus conservamur quam illi quibus nascimur, ...
profecto quoniam illum qui hanc urbem condidit, ad Deos im-
mortales benevolentia famaque sustulimus, esse apud vos pos-
terosque vestros in honore debebit qui eandem hanc urbem con-
ditam amplificatamque servavit." The founders of Amherst
College were many; but one man, pecuniarily speaking, rescued
it, preserved it, planted it anew on broader and deeper foundations, and has stood by it ever since to support and adorn it,
even though his contributions might bear the names of others.
His latest benefaction has just been announced. It is a birthday present to our mother—the handsome and appropriate gift of
fifty thousand dollars on her fiftieth anniversary—one thousand
dollars for every year of her life! Her children gratefully acknowledge the gift, and with one voice unite with her in the
prayer, God save the king—long live Samuel Williston!

But we must not fail to mention others who came to the relief
and support of the College during this administration—Samuel
A. Hitchcock, who, in completing the endowment of the Hitchcock professorship, only commenced the series of liberal donations which he has since extended and enlarged; Josiah B. Woods,
whose Cabinet was the first visible step upward under the new
regimen, in the improvement of the College buildings and
grounds, (long may that Cabinet escape the profane hands that
would level it with the chasm which now yawns by its side!)
and whose representation of the scientific merits of Dr. Hitchcock and the self-denial of his colleagues, not only won the
friendship of Abbot Lawrence and other benefactors, but pre-

8

pared the way for the conquest of the Legislature and the first grant they ever made to Amherst College; David Sears, whose "Foundation of Literature and Benevolence" has so long been the chief fountain of supply and increase to our library, and which, by the perpetual addition of one-half of the annual interest to the principal, is destined in future ages to become one of our richest as well as most beneficent foundations; Jonathan Phillips, whose donations to the library, next to those of David Sears, have brightened the eyes and gladdened the hearts of officers and students; George Merriam, who headed our subscription for the new library building with a generous donation; George C. Shepard, who was the largest subscriber in the effort of the alumni to replenish the building with books; Samuel Appleton, whose Ichnological Cabinet has made indelible *his* "foot-marks on the sands of time;" Charles U. Shepard and C. B. Adams, whose collections can not be estimated in money, and are of more value than the buildings in which they are deposited. We can not dwell on any of them, still less can we stop to magnify the consummate generalship, the weight of character and the personal influence by which those large accessions to the material of education were secured. Nor would Dr. Hitchcock himself allow us so to do. For with a modesty and Christian humility as remarkable as his wisdom, this great and good man regarded himself in all these measures as only the instrument of Divine Providence. And in his address on retiring from the presidency, he says: "It seemed to me as obviously God's work, as if I had seen the sun and moon stand still, or the dead start out of their graves; and it appeared as absurd for me to boast of my agency in the work, as for the wires of the telegraph to feel proud because electricity was conveying great thoughts through them. Oh, no, let the glory of this change be now and ever ascribed to a special Divine Providence."

If Dr. Humphrey was our Moses, the giver of our laws and institutions, Dr. Hitchcock was our Joshua, who led us into the promised land, conquered our enemies by making them friends, and gave us secure and permanent possession of houses that we did not build, and vineyards and olive yards that we planted not. It is not difficult to discern the distinctive features of this portion of our history. It was in many respects a new era, and that in no small measure the result of a new policy. It was the end—forever let us hope—of living beyond our means and running in debt. It was the end of general subscriptions to meet current expenses. It was the beginning of endowments by large donations from individuals. It was the beginning (and to all appearance nearly the end) of grants by the State. It was the age of growth and expansion in cabinets, collections and materials for the illustration of the physical sciences. At the same time, it was the period in which the foundations of our library were laid—the building and we might almost say the books. Last, not least, it inaugurated the reign of comparative peace. From its commencement, there was less of hostility abroad than there had ever been before, and more than for many years previous of peace, quietness, contentment and satisfaction at home. This was partly the result of a change of times and circumstances, and partly of a more paternal, perhaps we might say fraternal administration *suited* to the times. Yet there was no compromise with error or sin—no lowering of the standard of orthodoxy, evangelical piety, or any of the distinctive principles of the original founders. Temperance, revivals, missions, education of ministers, were still as conspicuous as ever on our banners.

The Professors and Tutors who were associated with Dr. Hitchcock in the government and instruction, were, for the most part, one with him in spirit; some of them added much to the lustre of his presidency, and were he to write the history of his own administration, he would ascribe a large share of its success to their hearty and able co-operation. But the larger part of them are still living—only three of them now connected with the College—the rest, for the most part, working and shining in the departments of education, letters, theology and religion elsewhere. Aaron Warner, Thomas P. Field, Henry B. Smith, Joseph Haven, George B. Jewett, David Torrey, Lewis Green, Marshall Henshaw, Francis A. March, Albert Tolman, William Howland, Henry L. Edwards, William C. Dickinson, George Howland, John Sanford, George N. Webber, —these are names now well-known to the public as well as familiar to the ears and dear to the hearts of many of us, and they represent not only the Faculty, but, for the most part, the alumni also, of this period. But it remains for those who come after us and outlive them, to give their character and write their history.

Six of Dr. Hitchcock's colleagues in the Faculty—three Professors and three Tutors—have gone to participate with him in the honors and rewards of faithful service. The three Professors all departed in advance of their honored and beloved President. One, a ripe scholar and veteran Professor, went up from the city where our Lord was crucified, to walk the streets of the New Jerusalem. His body rests beneath an olive-tree on Mount Zion, and methinks his spirit looks down with sacred joy upon the prosperity of his beloved College, for which he labored and prayed and hoped to the end, but died just before the tide of success began to return into the old channels. Another, who seemed born for a collector and classifier of all facts in natural history, the youthful Aristotle of our Lyceum, went to the West Indies, partly for his health, but chiefly to enlarge his scientific collections, and there fell a sacrifice to his zeal for science when he had only just commenced his career of discovery, though he had already achieved more than many a savant accomplishes in a long life.

> "Oh, what a noble heart was here undone,
>   When Science's self destroyed her favorite son!
>   Yes, she too much indulged thy fond pursuit;
>   She sowed the seeds, but death has reaped the fruit!"

A third, scholarly and refined, full of hope and promise, had just entered his professorship, and just begun to inspire his class with his own enthusiasm for the language and the literature of the old Romans, when he was suddenly stricken down by the destroyer; and yet his death, awakening the thoughts and touching the hearts of his pupils, became to not a few of them a means of spiritual and eternal life. The religious life of William A. Peabody began in the revival of 1835, and ended, nay, began anew, was multiplied and perpetuated with that of 1850.

Of the three Tutors, Leonard Humphrey had made the mark of a fine scholar and a gentle Christian spirit on his pupils for one year, and was recruiting himself in vacation with his friends for the labor of a second year; but suddenly, in the midst of health and activity, he fell to the ground—his heart had ceased to beat—"he was not, for God took him." John M. Emerson lived to middle life, and lived to good purpose; for he had demonstrated to the conviction of all who knew him that an honest, cultivated Christian lawyer can live and succeed in New York; when, in the very prime of his life and promise, the bar of that city was robbed of so rare an ornament, and at the same time a widowed mother in Amherst bereft of her only son. Samuel Fisk had left his tutorship, had written his letters from foreign parts, all flashing with wit and genius, and by a few years of able and faithful service in the ministry, had already rooted

himself in the hearts of an affectionate people, when the clarion
of war summoned him to the tented field, and he fell in the
battle of Spotsylvania, one of many noble sons whom our
mother has given to the service of the country, of liberty and
of mankind.

When Dr. Hitchcock retired from the presidency to resume
his favorite scientific pursuits, the College was already placed
on a solid basis. What remained to be done was to enlarge
those foundations, of course, and build the superstructure higher
so as to keep pace with the progress of the age, but chiefly to
impart unity, completeness and finish to the work, to introduce
more of order and beauty into the buildings and the grounds,
to give the students a wider, more impartial and more symmet-
rical culture,—in short, to develop and apply a little more of the
æsthetic element in the architecture, horticulture, and education
of this "consecrated eminence," without detracting one iota
from its sacredness, without removing a single element of solid
and substantial excellence. How well this conscious want of
the Institution has been met, I need not say, for you can see
with your own eyes. "Si monumenta quæris, circumspice."
Look at the Barrett gymnasium, Williston Hall, the Walker
building and the College church. They are not only models of
architectural beauty and fitness, each for its own use and place,
but they are the outward signs and symbols of a higher art and
culture that have been introduced into all the departments of
education. The finished and furnished lecture-rooms, even in
the old chapel, are indexes of progress in the same direction.
Most of you will feel more at home in the old "Mathematical
room" which we have left just as it was made in 1827, on purpose that you might visit it and bring up the memory of olden
times. But as you go from that to the new Greek and Latin
and Philosophical rooms, and even to the large and small chapels,

we think, you will all acknowledge that the new is better. And if you would be assured that the new culture and refinement which these improvements indicate, have not been purchased at the expense of the discipline, virtue and Christian piety of the good old times, see a pledge in the very constitution of the Faculty, one of whose members has been connected with the College under all its successive administrations, and another under all but the first—this certainly does not look like a passion for change. Read a proof of the same thing in the wisely balanced system of ancient literature and modern science, of required and elective courses of study, put forth by the President, with the approbation of the Professors and the sanction of the Trustees, at the opening of Walker Hall. Take, as a further exponent, that significant and characteristic expression in the first sentence of the President's preliminary statement at the placing of the corner-stone of the College church: "The highest education, and all for Christ," which has become the motto of his administration. And see a more conclusive demonstration of the same fact in the mathematicians and scholars, as well as masters of modern science, literature and art that have been lately educated here, and the Christian teachers and preachers, recent graduates, who are to be found not only in every section of our own rapidly extending territory, but who are going forth from us every year to officer the Colleges and supply the missionary stations in distant lands. Yes, the same wise and kind Providence which has watched over the College from the beginning, and raised up the men that were needed for every emergency, when President Hitchcock resigned, provided just the leader that was wanted to supplement his work, to preserve, balance and polish the substance of all that was old, and adding much that was new, to carry on the work to perfection. And the younger members of the Faculty are in unison with the

President and the older members in regard to the principles
and measures of College government, the general system and
method of physical and mental education, and the paramount
necessity of moral and spiritual culture above all the highest
attainments of literature and science, while, at the same time,
they bring to the accomplishment of these common ends a
measure of zeal and enthusiasm, a breadth of culture and a
wealth of learning which could hardly be expected of their
older colleagues.   I say this, not because it is necessary, but
because it is just.   We who have been connected with the
Faculty during the larger part of the half century, so far from
feeling that the old was better, can truly and heartily say that
the Faculty has never been constituted so entirely to our satisfaction as now.   And while we look with the love and compla-
cency of a father upon all our children, the older as well as the
younger, and are perhaps too ready to assert more than our
proper share in the reputation of the great and good men we
have educated, saying to them as the aged Phœnix did to the
godlike Achilles :—

"All illustrious as thou art, I made thee such ; "
Καί σε τοσοῦτον ἔϑηκα θεοῖς ἐπεείκελ' Ἀχιλλεῦ ;

yet we must be allowed to cherish a little preference for the
children of our riper years, especially our youngest, our Benjamins, who are to graduate to-morrow ; even as the Germans,
however large their families may become, always say : "das
neueste, das beste"—the last is the best.

But this administration has not yet come to a close, and
therefore is not yet a proper subject of history.   Long may it be
before its history can be written.   Long may President Stearns
live to serve the College and to see the fruits of his wise and
faithful labors.

Of all the remarkable providences by which friends and benefactors, presidents and professors, men and means, have always been raised up to meet the necessities of the College, not the least remarkable, certainly, is that which secured to it the donations and bequests of Dr. Walker ; and of all the achievements of generalship or diplomacy which illustrate our annals, none is more brilliant than that by which the Doctor was taken captive and guided with easy rein and cautious hand till the prize was secured. Born in Charlestown, educated at Cambridge, having no geographical, social, educational or religious affinity with Amherst, he was, notwithstanding, led by unforeseen circumstances and wise influences to become its largest pecuniary benefactor, and to establish here foundations which, through the eye and the ear, by beautiful halls, learned professors and liberal scholarships, will educate noble youth in untold numbers till distant ages.

We are indebted for the College Church to the son of our President, a young man whose enterprise and diplomatic skill, while enriching himself and gathering means to enrich Amherst, at the same time opened a new channel for the commerce between India and England. Of unsurpassed beauty both in itself and in its situation, this building is destined to become— I will not say a new center for a new cluster of edifices crowning and encompassing the eastern brow of College Hill, as the old Chapel is the arx of the cluster on the western citadel—but, I will say, another focus of the ellipse or quadrangle of edifices that will one day, doubtless, enclose, and perhaps fill, the entire College campus, and that, too, probably, enlarged beyond even its now extended area.

While thus paying a deserved tribute to the memory of those who have given us our funds, we ought not to pass without mention those who have kept these funds for fifty years "without losing a dollar." I believe I have the best financial author-

9

ity in the Board of Trust for this statement in regard to the
present Treasurer, and, I am sure, it is equally true of his predecessor in office.   Deacon Leland (Deacon Termbill we students used sometimes irreverently to call him—for a very good
reason, the College Treasurer is not so much in favor with the
students as he is with the Professors ;) Deacon Leland, who was
Treasurer of the College for the first fifteen years on a salary
of two hundred and fifty dollars, never more than three hundred
dollars, and was also much of the time Commissioner of the
Charity Fund, member of the Prudential Committee, working
member of building committees, inspector of buildings and
grounds, collector of subscriptions, and general agent ; Deacon
Leland, I say, probably devoted more time to the external
affairs of the College, and certainly gave it more money out of
his own pocket than was ever given by any other citizen of Amherst, and well deserves a name and a place among the founders.   Lucius Boltwood, thirty-one years Commissioner of the
Charity Fund, and thirty-six years Secretary of the Corporation, still lives, and is present with us to-day, to commemorate,
in the eightieth year of his age, that opening of this Institution
on which he looked with such hopeful, yet anxious interest, fifty
years ago, the only resident of our village now living who was
in business or a profession here when the College was founded.
The alumni delight to honor him as a faithful servant of the
College, and the sole representative of a generation that has
passed away.

May the present incumbents of these two offices, the Treasurer and the Commissioner, live as long as their predecessors
have.   We have no doubt they will leave an equally good
record of able and faithful services to be recorded by the
historian of the next half century.

Alumni brothers, we are here to-day to celebrate the fiftieth anniversary of our mother's birth. We find her still in the bloom of youth, with every indication of more than usual health and happiness. She was never before in so comfortable circumstances; never before enjoyed so fully the love of her sons, the confidence and good-will of the whole community. She has more students this year than she has ever had; to-morrow she will send out, with her blessing, the largest class (one only excepted) that she has ever graduated. It was the largest, without exception, (I may say aside to the older children of our family,) till, in consequence of a higher standard, several members of the class were "graduated prematurely" at the end of the fall term. And we are here from every section of the country—from every quarter of the globe we are here to felicitate her, and to rejoice with her in all the auspicious circumstances of so happy an occasion. We come bringing our birthday presents, some more, some less, for we have not all been equally prosperous; none of them very large, for wealth is not the inheritance or the boast of our family, yet none the less acceptable to our Alma Mater as the expression of her children's love, and welcome also as the means of educating more such noble sons in coming years. But, more than all that they bring with them, she prizes her sons themselves. These are the jewels which she wears on her brow to-day—these the gems she carries in her hands and treasures in her heart.

The alumni of Amherst adorn every profession. The reverend clergy outnumber, and perhaps outshine, the other professions, for the education of ministers was the primary object for which the College was founded, and it has not proved false to the intention of its founders. But our young lawyers and physicians are rapidly rising to the same high rank in New York and Boston which our preachers have so long and so conspicuously held in Brooklyn, and more recently taken in other

cities.   Literature, also, and science, and theology, count Amherst graduates among their brightest ornaments.   They have
carried their knowledge and culture with them into the high
places of agriculture and manufactures, engineering and machinery, commerce and business of every kind.   The periodical
press owns their sway from Andover to San Francisco, in the
valley of the Connecticut and on the banks of the Hudson.
Next to religion, education is perhaps the sphere in which our
College has especially ruled, and her sons are to be found at
the head of Academies and High Schools without number, from
the farthest East to the far West, and officering Colleges, from
the Massachusetts Agricultural College in Amherst to the
Syrian College in Beyrut and the Robert College in Constantinople; from the oldest Theological Seminaries in this country
to the most recent schools for the education of native preachers and teachers in Turkey, India, China and Japan.   They
have not often sought distinction in political and public life,
but promotion has sometimes sought them, and they have honored and adorned the gubernatorial office in Massachusetts,
and the Speaker's chair in the Congress of the United States;
they have filled and illustrated some of the highest stations,
legislative, executive and judicial, in the state and the nation.

And when the great rebellion aimed a deadly blow at the national existence, graduates of Amherst, side by side with those
of other Colleges, bared their own breasts to receive the blow,
enlisted in the ranks, raised companies and regiments, marched
at the head of divisions, rushed into the imminent deadly
breach, fell in storming intrenchments, were killed on the field
of battle, died in hospitals and prisons, poured out their blood
like water for their country and mankind.   The older graduates
not only went themselves, but sent their sons to the fight.   A
member of the class of '29 writes: "I had four sons in the war,

two of them in nearly the whole of it. One of them, for about ten months, suffered deaths oft in rebel prisons. He saw Libby, Danville, Andersonville and Florence in that time." This is only a specimen. Ex uno disce omnes.

The under-graduates outstripped the graduates in their patriotic zeal and devotion. On that dark Sunday after the first disastrous battle, when it was feared that the Capital might already have fallen into the hands of the rebels, they formed a volunteer company, drew up articles of enlistment, and offered their services to the Governor, deeming it a Christian duty, not unbecoming the·Lord's day, to enlist in such a war, and at the same time adopting as their own the sentiment which they so much admired in their ancient classics: "Dulce et decorum est pro patria mori." The President's son was the first to put his name to this paper; a son of one of the Professors was the next to enter the lists. The former was one of the earliest sacrifices which our College offered on the altar of the country. He fell in the battle of Newbern just within the intrenchments, beckoning his men on to victory. One of our Professors commanded the regiment to which he belonged; and one of the enemy's field-pieces near which he fell, presented by the commanding General to the College, now stands in the vestibule of the library to commemorate the bravery of our brothers in that struggle and to animate those who come after us with a like spirit of self-sacrificing devotion. Scores of under-graduates thus relinquished the toga for the sword, till our classes, reduced in numbers, seemed almost like the thinned ranks of an army after a great battle. The "Roll" which Professor Crowell has prepared with so much labor and care, contains the names of two hundred and forty-seven graduates and under-graduates who served in the army or navy during the war; and thirty-four of these directly or indirectly sacrificed their lives in the service.

" Dead on the field of battle," is the response which we hear
from the lips of their comrades as we call the roll to-day.   They
need not the chime of memorial bells in yonder church to perpetuate the memory of their brave deeds and heroic sacrifices.
No, brothers, we will enshrine you in the memory of our hearts ;
louder and longer than the peal of bells shall your virtues sound
through the ages, and your example will stir those who come
after you to do and dare, to suffer, and if need be, to die in the
cause of liberty, humanity and religion.   Nor will those more
numerous and not less noble sons be forgotten, who, not in the
same manner, but in the same spirit of heroes and martyrs,
have toiled and suffered and died on the great moral and
spiritual battle-fields of the church and the world.   We can
not boast of the long line of Presidents and Governors and
Cabinet Officers and Ambassadors to foreign courts that have
marched down the generations and centuries in the history of
older Institutions.   But wherever there has been any great
battle to be fought, any prolonged and desperate war to be
waged, any hard work to be done at home or abroad, in civilized
or savage lands, for truth and justice, for liberty and humanity,
for learning and religion—there the sons of Amherst are sure to
be found, doing the hardest of the work, leading in the hottest
of the fight, the true working-men in the great field of the
world, brave soldiers in the service of the Son of Man and the
Son of God.   Such hitherto has been the history of Amherst
College—such be her fame and glory in all coming ages.

These funds that have been raised with so much difficulty,
are valuable.   These collections which have been gathered with
so much labor and science, are precious.   These rooms and
halls where we have studied and prayed, these groves and
grounds where we have walked and talked, are all hallowed by
sacred associations, and will only grow more sacred as we visit

them from one decennary to another as long as we live. But these are not Amherst College, any more than these frail and decaying bodies are ourselves. Sooner or later the funds will all be dissipated, the collections will be scattered, the walls will crumble and disappear, and this consecrated eminence, with all the material beauty and glory that crown it and encompass it on every side, will change and pass away. But the men that have taught and studied here, the educators and the educated, the presidents and professors and students, are immortal. The lessons of wisdom and duty that have been inculcated and learned here, the characters that have been formed, the work that has been done, the victories that have been achieved, and the moral and spiritual results that have been accomplished—these are our history; these have been inwrought into our minds and hearts, and through us into the minds and hearts of others; these have been incorporated with the history of mankind and the kingdom of God, and they will be eternal. These will be a part of that universal history of education and redemption which the wise and good will read and recount to each other in the jubilees of heaven, and which teachers and pupils will study together and see in lights ever new and ever fresh, as they sit at the feet of the Great Teacher, "in whom are hid all the treasures of wisdom and knowledge."

After the close of Professor Tyler's discourse, the Society of Alumni was called to order by Hon. A. B. Ely, President, for the transaction of the customary business.

In the afternoon, at two o'clock, the assembly gathered again under the tent, and were addressed by Hon. A. H. Bullock, who had been chosen to preside, Professor Snell, Rev. Dr. E. P. Humphrey, Rev. H. N. Barnum, Rev. H. W. Beecher, Professor Park, Professor R. D. Hitchcock and Waldo Hutchins, Esq.

The speeches expected from Professor H. B. Hackett, Bishop Huntington, Hon. H. S. Stockbridge, George Clark, Esq., and Willard Merrill, Esq., the delivery of which was prevented, from lack of time, have been prepared, and are herewith presented.

AFTERNOON SESSION.

ADDRESS OF GOV. BULLOCK.

Fellow-students, Alumni of Amherst: I take the chair which has been assigned to me by your partiality, rather felicitating myself in the custom which limits with a stern propriety the remarks of the presiding officer, and throws the silver gate of speech wide open only to the assembly. Our *Alma Mater* is just now passing the threshold of one of the notable historic stages you are here to witness and commemorate, and everything you please is in order—except silence. Nor is it within my authority to impose any limitations upon the strings of your harpsichords. Your strain may be Doric, Æolian, robust, tender, serious, comic, as you prefer ; remindful of a student-lamp, or of moonlight among the fields and groves, of a four years' wrestle for a college honor, or of dalliance with the purest carnation in the cheeks of the village—all as you please, save only that it is of Amherst you are to speak. Let us then hail this hour without any reserve. The weightier duties of the day have already been performed by the historian, in the delivery of his comprehensive and elaborate address. He has won the battle for the College by his heavy artillery, and we may vote ourselves a sort of light-horse squadron, whose part it is to appropriate the victory and carry away the plunder.

10

For myself, it is but few words I would say.   I have no passion to tear to tatters in behalf of the occasion, no conception
beyond my little capacity of utterance, no historical sweep
which overcomes or confuses me.   I am here only to utter the
testimony of a witness, the experience of a son, and the prophecy of one who foresees the glory of the coming day.   I came
here a Freshman of sixteen, thirty-nine years ago, exercising my
own volition in coming, and I can now look you in the face and
declare that from that day to this I have never for one moment
regretted the choice I made.   I have grown up with this College, never having seen any reason to abate my respect or at-
tachment, and if I could live a thousand years there would be
one son who should make the periodical visit of filial piety to
her halls.   But though I can not add to the length of my days,
I rejoice that the duration of hers is assured.   The types of her
immortality are impressed upon our sight.   This Institution
was planted amid the grandeurs 'and beauties of our own
Switzerland, which can not pass away save with the globe itself.
This Institution was founded in the broad beliefs of the Christian world, which are imperishable.   This Institution has developed and will continue to develop in the light of those humani-
ties which survive individualities and generations, and belong
to the eternal years of God.   It holds a place among the certainties of our land.   It is in fraternal accord with all the Colleges of every State and of every faith; it takes as a magnet to
every improvement, from whatever quarter it may come, and is
receptive to every inspiration of science or art, as the world is
to-day and shall be afterwards; it seats the rich and the poor at
the same table of a common study and love; it estimates every
man coming within its influence by the dignity of his divine
relations, and espouses the duty of his education as a trust to
be executed in the highest responsibility of which human na-

ture is capable. Around such an Institution endowments and supports will rally with increasing measure, still augmenting numbers of young men will seek its benefits, and its expansion and embellishment is among the sure events of the future. It is a result of the labors of the builders that can not decay, because they builded on the chief corner-stone.

I doubt if any other of the American colleges, in its first fifty years, has educated so many men, or contributed so largely to the culture and manliness of the people, to the grace and defense of the State. Its infancy was a brief one, and it rose at once to the proportions of vigorous manhood. When I came here, only eleven years after it had conferred its first degrees, I found in my own class rising of seventy, and in the Institution more than two hundred members. It was even then a growth, "past the gristle and hardened into the bone." When I cast a look backward to those who thronged the lecture rooms of that day, in whose ranks a discerning teacher might well think he saw

A little bench of heedless bishops here,
And there a chancellor in embryo ;—

for we now know that such were here,—and when I now look abroad upon what they have accomplished in all the fields of the public service, of original thought and useful art, of liberty and law, of religion and justice, of eloquence and mercy in all lands, and summon their faces before me, some now present but more absent, the living and the dead, and count up their names and their fame, I feel justified in pronouncing that period, which was the youth of the College, good as the golden age of any college. During these past fifty years the students here have had both the advantage and disadvantage of a new and young institution, —for in such a condition there is undoubtedly both a gain and a loss. The loss is of the long and gentle train of associated traditions, which in an ancient university passes from one generation of students to another, bearing the influence of accumulated fellowships, examples and cultures, and enriching the atmosphere of the modern time with the mellow light of the old. At Eton, at Oxford, at Cambridge on both sides of the ocean, these are sources of inspiration to the successive throngs of student life. So the nations of the old world have inspiring histories of a thousand years to guide and elevate the later generations by inherited lessons and admonitions. But as a new nation strikes boldly out in the marches of civilization, free of the superstitions and errors of the former, and bears onward the standard of progress and humanity to higher elevations than had been attained by the preceding, in somewhat similar manner and spirit the younger schools of learning may perhaps mount upward with steps lightened of the shackles of prescriptive custom, abuse and fallacy, and reach forward toward the prizes with less of the obstruction of rote and bias and prejudice. A young College is apt to be earnest in its work. So we have found ours to be. Our corps of Professors have been men of hard work, and the classes in every year of the course have received from them in person direct and constant instruction. I challenge your concurrence in the declaration that there has been as little nonsense and folly taught here as in any seminary of all our American Sion. We have sought to retain the classical inspirations of the past, and to make them tributary to the necessities of the solemn, living world. And now, at the close of such a first half century, we are willing that our College should be judged. By her origin and life, by her motive and purpose, by her efforts and achievement, by her sons who have borne her name into every part of the globe, such as they all have been, and such as they are who survive to speak her praise, we are willing that our *Alma Mater* should be judged.

You will agree with me in a moment of indulgence in pleasing personal memories. There is to many of you, as there is to me, the grateful recollection of having enjoyed the familiar confidence of the second and the third President of Amherst, both not long since ascended to their rest. The names of Heman Humphrey and Edward Hitchcock have an enduring place in the public annals, but their shrine is in the hearts of nearly two thousand students they taught. Of the former of these I desire to say, as a simple act of justice to his memory, that he filled the most important office in the most critical stage of the Institution, with a judgment and discretion that warrants me in calling him our foremost benefactor. A remarkably good teacher he was, also, a philosopher of profound thought, an orator sometimes attaining a brilliant eloquence. Another good he conferred. Out of this College he gave his own sons to the country, who have impressed the pulpit, the forum, the national councils, with a culture even broader than his own. I shall revere his memory through life. Of President Hitchcock still less need be said to-day, as the trumpet of fame has blown more widely his name. In him there was singular genius. How exquisitely his sensitive organization was strung—how delicate his perception was of all poetic and beautiful things—how he rose from the details of his science, of which he was master, into generalization and rhapsody upon its universal relations—how simple and modest in every sphere, ever self-distrustful and never self-satisfied—how kind, obliging, deferential to young men, we all remember, as we remember in equal degree of no one beside. He is a central figure in any grouping which our imagination may array under this canopy,—standing among us in that imperial form so long and so well known to all persons here, so disguising the benevolence and gentleness of his nature behind those glasses of intense green that he seemed inaccessible, "but to those men that sought him, sweet as summer." His name carried that of the College to the remotest part of the Union. The Trustees of Amherst, the inhabitants of this village, are incapable of a just and full appreciation of the common debt they owe to him. And of the living—not even the great delicacy of such speech shall deter me from selecting, for special mention to your ears, Professors Snell and Tyler, who have been connected with duty here through the lapse of forty years. They have made their mark upon the age, which neither forgetfulness of pupils nor length of time shall ever erase. Every generous impulse of my youth had dried away from my heart, if I had forgotten to ask you to bestow upon them your grateful plaudits. Nor would any personal allusions be adequate or just which should not specially point to the able and accomplished gentleman who now presides over the College,—his administration illustrated alike by the spirit of a scholar and the talent of an executive officer. I hope that it may be many more years that his various attainments, agreeable manners and firm hold of the helm shall be continued to the school he has with so much cordiality and devotion adopted. And those patrons—Williston, Walker, Hitchcock, many, many others—if you seek *their* monument, look around!

It is not for me in these words of salutation, which must not cut you off from your opportunity for speech—it is not for me to enter upon any detail of the future wants of the Institution, of what may be most essential or most expedient of policies or ways or means for keeping even march with the advancements of this era. I avoid debate upon the curriculum, past, present and future. I say only one thing, touching the whole matter ;— WE MUST ALL ACCEPT THE SITUATION. Our first half century is now behind us. We now diverge from the past to the future. Then we must keep time with the music and the tramp of the future.

It is worse than unavailing to hide, or complain, or sulk in these rapid days, which after all are the best days mankind have ever seen. Steam, stationary and locomotive, the electric currents coursing over land, under seas and through our own sensations, the hidden riches of the earth disgorged as never before to facilitate and intensify the agencies and activities of human life, all the useful and æsthetic arts, all the social and casuistic problems which agitate and quicken the mind;—these impose upon you and upon me, and especially upon the custodians of the Colleges, a responsibility which demands the combined wisdom of age and youth. Age alone will hesitate and falter; youth left to itself might go astray. Both, in rarest combination and harmony, are needed. I have no fears that any of the questions of scientific and practical courses of study, often treated as coming into conflict with the classical, will result either in disaster to our career or in confusion to our senses ; for it is already as well settled that the two must prosper together under equal endowment and encouragement, as it is settled that there has been a grand, sublime world in the past, and that there is a more beneficent and magnificent world in the present. That question will take care of itself. The more real questions which concern this epoch relate to the organic and elemental rights and duties of the constituent members of society. And at this moment, when men and parties are talking of new departures in other fields of action, there comes before us in the pathway of our Institution of education something that can not be turned aside, that may as well be confronted, whether it be a substance or a spectre. I would treat it as a substance. I allude to the question of the admission of the two sexes to an equality of privilege and benefit in the higher seminaries of learning throughout New England. Theory and argument appear to preponderate in favor of the proposition, and to be supported by whatever semblance of natural right there is to be found in such a case as that. The test of experience alone is partially wanting—but I think we have usually found that experience is somewhat accommodating to theory, and follows gracefully in the train of argument and truth. For one, I am in favor of closing the debate and taking the question, so far as we here are concerned with it. I am cordially in favor of making the experiment of admitting our friends heretofore excluded, to the privileges of the classes, if they shall desire it, and shall establish the usual qualifications. Nor, in my judgment, is it at all improbable that the class-rooms would be greatly improved by the new accession. Some one, writing of Raphael, said that his pencil melted whenever it approached a woman or an angel. I am not able to see why such influences may not profitably be transfused through the austere forms of the collegiate recitation room. At all events, I have sealed my opinion. And as the committee of arrangements have very properly been drumming through all the classes of fifty years standing or less in quest of the establishment of scholarship funds, as a fit memorial tribute to the occasion, I have sent in to my associates of the Board of Trustees my humble offering of a scholarship endowment, with the condition that its benefits shall be appropriated to a woman upon the basis of equal fitness in the examination. In that direction it is offered—and may Heaven grant it a blessing.

My fellow-students, the occasion is for much serious reflection as well as social rejoicing. We have many departed and beloved to lament; but the moving procession in life will not stay in mourning. We pay the passing tribute at every grave of a classmate, and resume our walk in the paths of the living. In those paths we, in our turn, soon shall fall, and may fondly hope for only the same momentary honors. This age is so crowded with men, with thick coming events, with engineries and forces in ceaseless motion, that the individual person is lost sight of when he ceases to act. Yet in all this scene of modern life, each one of us still retains his individuality and responsibility. Each one of us will still hold to the last his own circle of taste and affection. And in the waning years, let it be one of our aims and one of our consolations to keep bright the golden cincture that binds us to this home of our youth. I like the custom at Harvard of having a message of remembrance at every recurring anniversary from its oldest living alumnus. The college and the son can never part in life. If it be possible that the last days of the scholar shall become dreary, then, even then, he may draw solace and cheerfulness from this dwelling of his boyhood, from this association of his *Alma Mater* with himself. As he descends along the vale, and other associations give way, he may still address to her his invocation and hope :—

> "Be thou the rainbow to the storms of life !
> The evening beam that smiles the clouds away,
> And tints to morrow with prophetic ray !"

11

PROFESSOR SNELL'S ADDRESS.

Mr. President and Brothers, Alumni of Amherst College: As
I am one of the oldest of Amherst's sons, and have always staid
here at the homestead, it may not be out of place for me to join
the worthy President of our College, and say to you, old and
young, one and all,—Welcome to the old home.

I take it for granted that you are all good men and true, and
are faithfully performing some creditable life-work ; but if there
is among you all some prodigal son returning to receive the
maternal blessing on this occasion, I do not think the elder son
will take offense and refuse to meet him, even if our loving
parent should order the fatted calf to be killed for the poor
fellow.   No, we are glad to see *all* the boys ; I will not say
good, and *bad*, but *good*, and *better*, and *best*.   For if you conducted yourself well when in College, of course we are glad to
greet you as you come back again ; if you did not, we will presume that you have made the improvement which there was
room for.   I say then to every son of our Alma Mater, welcome
home on this happy semi-centennial.

If we use the civil reckoning of time, Amherst College is not
quite fifty years old.   Strictly, her birthday does not occur till
the 19th of September.   But, according to the *College* calendar,
in which the year begins and ends with Commencement, a calendar which we are obliged to employ instead of the *Gregorian*,
she is fifty years old this week.   Well, then, on Wednesday,

fifty years ago to-day, a number of young men presented themselves at the door of Amherst College, which had never been opened for any one to enter, and asked to be admitted. I was one of those young men,—and *I* asked admission to Senior standing. The door was opened, and we were received ; and *my* turn came first by about half a day. For I had closed my Junior year at Williams College, and had passed my examinations in the presence of Dr. Moore, who was President there, and had just been inaugurated President here ; and on his recommendation I was admitted at once, while all other applicants were obliged to wait till their examinations were closed before they could enter. At evening our College could number nearly sixty members, arranged in four classes, as shown in the first "Catalogue of the Collegiate Institution" at Amherst. *Then* I lacked a few days of being twenty years old. *Now*, I am almost three-score years and ten. This occasion tells me, as my friends are often telling me, that I am an old man, and I am becoming quite accustomed to the appellation. I suppose I ought to feel some infirmities; but here is just where I fail. I am not conscious of any infirmities, except the numerous ones which have always attended me. It may be supposed that I am mature enough to put on spectacles ; but I do not yet see clearly any good reason for doing so. And as to a cane, I have had any number of canes presented to me. The *gift* I always accept, but I never take the *hint.* It is possible, however, that the sophomoric weakness may yet fall upon me, and that I shall appear abroad with all my canes at once. I perform my College work with as much ease and interest as I ever did. And, really, I feel some solicitude lest I shall not know when to resign, unless some one tells me.

I have to meet almost all the graduates of this College as my former pupils. The interesting relation of pupil and teacher, which you and I once sustained toward each other, has ceased, never to be renewed. But the effects of this relationship, whether good or evil, will never cease. I wish I could have done my work better for you than I did. I ask you to overlook my deficiencies ; my faults I pray you to forgive.

Permit me to say a word respecting the gentleman who has recently endowed the scholarship of the first class,—the class of 1822. The gentleman is Wells Southworth, Esq., of New Haven, Conn. There is another *first* thing which he did for Amherst College. When it was proposed to the citizens of Amherst and neighboring towns to bring in their personal offerings of material and labor for a College building, Mr. Southworth, then a young man living in Pelham, went home, yoked up his father's oxen, and brought upon this hill a load of Pelham granite,—the very first load of material which was collected here for the erection of a College edifice. Those granite blocks are now in the foundations ·of the old South College. And now the same gentleman has laid another foundation stone, whose present nominal value is *one thousand dollars*, but whose real worth in the centuries to come it is beyond our power to estimate.

I did hope I might have the pleasure of introducing to you the other half of the living members of the class of 1822. That other half is the *first* half, the *oldest* half, the *greatest* half, and the *best* half. I refer to the Rev. Pindar Field of Hamilton, N. Y. He has lately sent word that, on account of illness, he cannot be present. I regret very much that you are not to hear a few words from him.

I close with the salutations with which I began,—a sincere and hearty welcome from the brothers at home to the brothers who have come in from abroad, on this our mother's fiftieth birthday.

ADDRESS BY REV. DR. E. P. HUMPHREY.

Mr. Chairman and Fellow-Students: Your Committee of Arrangements have requested me to respond for the administration of our second President. This duty would have been more gracefully discharged by another alumnus. But I do not feel at liberty to refuse the office, although hedged about with many limitations of delicacy and propriety. These limitations, however, are somewhat reduced by the fact that we may be said to occupy, to-day, towards President Humphrey's term of service the relation of posterity. He was inaugurated in October, 1823—forty-eight years ago ; and he retired from office in April, 1845, twenty-six years ago. That is the measure of time. But according to the wider measure of progress in society and of the changes wrought by many and great revolutions, in peace and war, we are removed to a period very remote from that presidency. Longer as well as

"Better fifty years of Europe, than a cycle of Cathay."

In this circumstance, I find an apology, at least, for responding to the call now made upon me.

It requires the effort of a mind that can recall not only, but can recreate the past, to set before us the year 1823. At that time the railroad, the steamship, the magnetic telegraph, and the gold mines of California were among the undiscovered forces of our material civilization. The marvels of machinery, which have imparted a prodigious impulse to the manufacturing industry of the country, were then unknown. The beginning of Dr. Humphrey's administration carries us back to the latter days of primitive times, when the vigorous old was ready to bring forth the more vigorous new. The old Puritan customs and traditions were still in vogue. The proverbs and maxims of the seventeenth century were current, and were quoted in the old-time accent and pronunciation. The Sabbath day was remembered to keep it holy. Thanksgivings, and fast-days, and town-meetings, and general trainings, and election days, and the shorter catechism, and doctrinal sermons running into the second hour, and the primeval Federal and Democratic parties held their own. We had no city in Massachusetts; it was the town of Boston. The roads leading thither from the west, climbed all the hill-tops from the Taconics to the sea. Highways they were, along which we toiled through the live-long day, leaving Boston a little after midnight, and reaching Northampton or Springfield a little before bed-time. But our journey was marked off and relieved by the dear old meeting-houses, posted on all the dividing ridges, by a sort of unconscious response to the piety of the ancient tribes, who erected altars at the headsprings of their rivers. The College was the product of that period; so, also, was its second President.

But we must take another step. Nothing is better known respecting the hard-working farmers of that day, than their desire to send their sons to College. Mr. Curtis, in his life of Daniel Webster, informs us that Captain Webster mortgaged his farm to educate his son Daniel, and then that he gave all that he had left to educate his son Ezekiel. Mr. Curtis might have added that similar parental sacrifices have been made a thousand times in those regions. A large proportion of the students of this College—I speak now of its first quarter century—were drawn from the farm-houses of these old hill towns, and were educated here by the toils and sacrifices of the father and the mother—and I might add the sisters and brothers,—working hard and long. When those came to Amherst in their homespun, they found here a President who knew all about the life of a penniless boy. He was himself the son of a small farmer, one of eleven children. This son labored on his father's farm till he was nearly grown. Then for about seven years, he served in summer as "hired man" on the farms of his neighbors, and in the winter he taught their children in the district schools. At the age of twenty-five he entered the Junior class in Yale College, supporting himself while there by waiting in the commons, and by teaching school; graduating honorably with his class, having paid all his College bills from the fruits of his own labor and economy, and leaving New Haven—such is the tradition—with nearly a hundred dollars in his pocket. This was the manner of man to whom our plain farmers and laboring people sent their sons when they sent them here, a man who knew more than they did about early poverty and the way to meet it; a man who had stood on every plank of the steep, arduous stairway that leads to Mr. Webster's upper story.

But we must go deeper than that. We must not lose sight of the fact that the College was established avowedly and undoubtedly for the purpose of educating men for the ministry of the gospel. It opened its doors from the beginning to every youth who sought a classical education, but its first and leading purpose was to raise up a company of men who should go into all the world, preaching the gospel. In 1823 they needed a President who was in the fullest accord with the enterprises in which the people of God, in and out of New England, were then engaging. In Dr. Humphrey, the Church recognized one of the founders of the American Bible Society; a supporter, from the beginning, of the American Board of Foreign Missions; as far back as 1811, an advocate of total abstinence as the infallible cure of intemperance; and as early as 1818, a friend of colonization, as the best remedy then proposed for African slavery. In him, also, what we call the "revival spirit," was a living power. His experience in several illustrious works of grace in Berkshire—works which changed the face of society there—gave him preparation to labor in the powerful revivals of religion which occurred here during his administration. They were six in number. They were so distributed through his term of service, that every class during its course of study, witnessed at least one of these displays of saving mercy. So genuine and enduring were their results, that a large majority of the students entered on the religious life, and of the seven hundred and ninety-five who were graduated by President Humphrey, four hundred and thirty became ministers of the gospel.

Our second President was in lively sympathy with the progress of society. He was a man of both the old and the new, not clinging to error because it was old, nor afraid of the true because it was new. It ought to be mentioned, that as far back as 1828, an elective course of study was established here, very similar to the scientific department now so common in other Colleges. The course proposed here differed from those now adopted, mainly in the fact that the elective course terminated in the bachelor's degree. It was abandoned here, partly for the want of funds, and partly, perhaps, because the public was not quite ready for it. But it was the beginning of that method of education, and owed its origin to the sagacity and enterprise of our second President and his associates.

For the rest, the College called into its service in him, a man of vigorous physical constitution, matured, not broken, by the

hardships of early years, of a sound common sense, and of a remarkable directness of purpose. With what courage and success
he fought out your early battles with penury and discontent, with
loud detraction and faint praise, with hot enemies and cold friends,
let the old men around me tell you. Through it all he was calm,
resolute, hopeful, full of mother wit, not in the habit of being
baffled or put down, not easily scared or hurt; and, above all, be-
lieving in God. They say he was somewhat stern at times, in his
methods of discipline. But so was his master, Timothy Dwight,
and so were his contemporaries, Jeremiah Day, Edward Dorr
Griffin, John Thornton Kirkland, and Josiah Quincy. Perhaps,
also, the boy-nature of that generation was less self-willed and
unruly than the boy-nature of this softer and gentler age! But it
must be said that he left to the College no injurious custom or
precedent or tradition—not one. And further, it is to be said that
neither by word or act, not even by a hasty word or an impulsive
act, whether in anger or merriment, did this man leave upon
any one of his thousand pupils an impression derogatory to the
honor or integrity or manners of a Christian gentleman.

It is a well-known tradition that Massachusetts has sought
tranquillity under liberty by the sword. But for the perfection and
perpetuity of that tranquillity she is indebted to the pious labors
of such men as Moore and Humphrey and Hitchcock and
Stearns, and their associates here, and their contemporaries in
the colleges and churches of Massachusetts. I speak in the
presence of the leading citizens of the Commonwealth, her scholars and jurists and clergymen and statesmen,—in the presence of
our distinguished Chairman, who has already adorned the Chair
of State, and he touches nothing that he does not adorn. In
this superb presence I repeat the sentiment uttered by our second
President when he retired from office, " My hope for the colleges,
for my country and the church, is in God."

12

ADDRESS BY REV H. N. BARNUM.

SIX weeks ago, when I came to Constantinople, on my long journey from beyond the Euphrates, I found a good number of the sons of Amherst at the annual meeting of the Western Turkey Mission. The day before I left they held an informal meeting, at which they commissioned me to bear to their Alma Mater and to the alumni, their most cordial and affectionate greetings, and to assure them of their continued interest in the College, and of their prayers for her success.

The representatives of this College, who are laboring in the Turkish Empire, are so numerous and doing so important a work in the regeneration of the country as to justify a brief mention of some of them.

The oldest class represented is that of '29, by Dr. Riggs. You know we live near the seat of the ancient Babel, and so have a good many of the languages represented there. Dr. Riggs is more or less familiar with most of the languages of Western Asia and of Europe, and whenever it becomes necessary for him to learn a new language, he makes about as little of it as some of us do in learning a new tune. His great work has been the translation of the Scriptures. He has given the Bible to the Armenians in the modern language, in a style so pure and clear as to dignify the language of common life and overcome the prejudices of the people against it, and secure its use in literature in the future—thus doing for the

Armenians just what Luther did for the Germans. This same work he has just done for the millions of Bulgarians in European Turkey. The last page of the Bulgarian Bible was printed while I was in Constantinople this time—the completion of a great work. Dr. Riggs has also aided somewhat in the translation and revision of the Scriptures in the Turkish language, and during the coming year he will probably assist in preparing the New Testament in Koordish for the press. In addition to all this, and to a good deal of general missionary work, he has done more for the hymnology of the Armenians than any other man—having translated a large number of the most beautiful of our own matchless hymns, preserving almost all the delicacy of the original. He has done a great work—one upon which any man might look with satisfaction.

The class of '30 has two representatives. The Pope falsely claims to be the successor of Peter, but we have a genuine successor of the Apostle Paul in Mr. Powers, who is laboring at Antioch. In addition to his ordinary missionary work, he has put a good many hymns into the Turkish, and now, by vote of his mission, he is to revise the Turkish Hymn Book.

Dr. Schneider, of the same class, after having gathered the largest congregation and the largest church in Turkey, at Aintab, is now laboring in Broosa. He has acquired the Turkish language so as to be able to use it with all the fluency and elegance of an educated Turk, and so far as my observation goes, he is the most eloquent preacher in Turkey.

In Constantinople we have the two brothers Bliss. Dr. Edwin of '37, though in poor health, sends out his weekly Messenger freighted with moral, religious and scientific instruction, to thousands of readers in both the Armenian and Turkish languages, and its corner of political intelligence is the standard in any doubtful matter, among men of all classes,

Christian and Turk, because they distrust their own papers, but they know that the "Avedaper" will not lie.

His brother Isaac of '44, the agent of the American Bible Society, is a man of irrepressible energy. He has given an impulse to the Bible work which is felt from the Nile to the Danube and Black Sea, and from the Bosphorus to the Caspian. He is now superintending the erection of a Bible House in Constantinople—the gift of American Christians to the East— which is to be a center of light and blessed influence for all that part of the world.

From my own class—'52, Allen, my own associate at Harpoot, is laying foundations on the Euphrates and Tigris, and, as Principal of the Theological Seminary, he is helping to raise up a large corps of native preachers and pastors.

At Beirut, Bliss of the same class, is President of the College, and he is laboring with might and main to prepare educated men for the one hundred and twenty millions who speak the Arabic. In this he is aided by Lewis and Porter of later classes.

So, too, on the Bosphorus, Washburn of '55 is associated with Dr. Hamlin in the care of Robert College, and is educating representatives of the various races and languages in that region. Grosvenor of '67 assists him in this work.

Then there are Clarke and Locke in Bulgaria, Bartlett at Cesarea, Hitchcock at Constantinople, and Cole at Erzroom all good men and true, and all doing a work which is to abide.

The "Eastern Question" has been several times settled, but like Banquo's ghost, it "will not down." The Sultan and his ministers plan, the protecting powers in Europe instruct their ambassadors and hold conferences and fix up affairs, but like the sword of Damocles, the Eastern Question ominously hangs over Turkey and all Europe, threatening the peace of all. But more potent than princes and statesmen is that band of quiet Christian laborers who are introducing the Gospel leaven. This is the leaven which is to leaven the lump. The Gospel brings education and civilization in its train, and prepares men for freedom, and the Eastern Question will never receive a *permanent* settlement till the missionary problem is wrought out.

This is recognized by Christian Englishmen. When I came to London a few days ago, I was almost overwhelmed by the attentions of great and good men, simply because I was a missionary from Turkey. When I consented, on two occasions, to speak in public, the bare announcement that I was an American and a missionary, drew out from the audience enthusiastic applause. After one of my addresses, I was followed by Lord Shaftsbury, who, after pronouncing one of his extravagant encomiums upon American missionaries, appealed to Englishmen, in the light of the new treaty, to join Americans in the great work of the world's redemption. He said: "Now that mercy and truth have met together and righteousness and peace have kissed each other, it behooves America and England, the two great Protestant nations, having one faith and one language, to join hands in every noble enterprise, and to hasten the day when all shall yield allegiance to the Savior."

In speaking of our own Alumni, I would not forget the representatives of the many other Colleges who are laboring with equal fidelity; but as the sons of Amherst constitute about one-fourth of the whole missionary force in the Turkish Empire, they are, taken together, more prominent than any others. And here, as I call to mind the toils and tears and sacrifices by which this College has been brought to its present position, I confidently affirm that if it had done nothing more in the world than what it has done, is doing, and is bound to do for

Turkey, it is an ample return. Her sons are regenerating the Empire. They are founding a Christian kingdom which shall stand till the trump shall sound. They are restoring Christianity in the land of its birth—where Christ suffered and where apostles labored and preached. The kingdom of God *is* coming, perhaps not "with observation," but it is surely coming and is yet to prevail. The same is also true of other lands besides Turkey. In every country where missionaries have gone, you will find the sons of Amherst among them.

And now, we wish to pledge this College anew to this work. We need, for the different fields, twenty or thirty of the very best of the Alumni of the last fifteen years—not those who have failed in the pastorate—if such there be—but men of the best talent, most varied culture and greatest energy, who have succeeded in life and proved their ability. This College is the Lord's. It was founded for Him. I rejoice in all the evidences which I see of its prosperity, but prosperity is apt to beget worldliness. Better far the trials and discouragements of thirty years ago, if prosperity is to separate her from Christ. Better that our brethren should be hewers of wood and drawers of water for the Temple which Christ is building, than mere selfish worldlings in Senate or presidential halls. For he who strikes a blow for Christ does a work which is to abide. You who hold these interests in charge, have a difficult task to resist the encroachments of the world and of unbelief, but we who stand upon the outposts expect to be strengthened from here, and we urge you to be faithful. Amherst has no more loyal sons than her missionary children. We pledge you our sympathy and our prayers. We have little else to give. Our constant prayer is that the blessing of God may daily rest upon you and upon the College. God bless our Alma Mater. May her future be even more conspicuous for Christian service than the past.

REV. H. W. BEECHER'S ADDRESS.

Before I speak for myself, let me protest at this unmannerly way the Chairman has of dropping, as he says, from one class to another. Beginning some fifteen years before me, they were not very smart then, and by the time you get to my class I shall be a natural born fool. I shall attempt, however, to maintain my equanimity by not listening to him, especially to those heretical sentiments he advanced on woman education.

I hold in my hand a letter which represents a gentleman, one whom I should not love better if he had sucked at the same breast, one who has served his apprenticeship as a scholar, who has been invoked, I believe, to take up servitude in the Faculty, but declined, who has not hesitated to give his best strength and time to aid the Trustees,—I mean one of the most brilliant scholars, and one of the best men we have in America, I mean Richard Salter Storrs. His long and severe labors so far undermined his health that his people sent him abroad to rest from a year to a year and a half. I will read a few sentences and then a line or two which refers to this occasion.* The rest is a love letter to Dr. Stearns.

Mr. Chairman and Gentlemen: All of my life long I have been moved to take the weaker side. I have heard the old Presidents praised, not a bit too much; and I have heard sundry members of the Faculty praised, and not a particle too

---

* The letter is appended.

much ; and I have heard Amherst praised almost *ad nauseam.*
But since I appealed to that principle, I have not heard a word
as yet, of what we poor fellows have to say who were in the
College, and under these Professors and Presidents. Why,
when I look to my own misery, I cannot conceive of any other
to equal it, unless it was the teachers that had to do with me.
First came that universal and mysterious trembling with which
I approached the hour of examination. What examination
meant, I did not know. But I thought I would be transfixed
or translated,—at any rate, the translation was what I most
dreaded. That ordeal was safely passed, and I came very
speedily under the hands of Professor Peck. The name is not
a just and proper expression of the containing quantities.
What I suffered in being made a ripe and ready Latin scholar,
nobody can imagine but him. His health failed soon after.
Since that time he has improved, and he is here to-day, looking
as young as I am. I think that nowhere were the steps of ambitious youth spurred and guided with greater alacrity than
mine. In my study of Greek, under Professor Fiske, I felt that
every special hair of his head was a spur, and I had the benefit
of them all. That has always seemed to me the reason why I ex-
celled in that more than in any other department of the College,
unless it was in mathematics. One thing I am certain, that Professor Snell never made so many original demonstrations as
I did. He would only demonstrate Euclid when it was all in a
book ; I liked to do things originally, and I did. There is one
thing that I can say, that he strove to be a pure and upright
man, but the feeling of envy was not wanting in those days in his
bosom. One thing I know, and that is, toward the close of my
course in his department,—whether it was from jealousy or not,
he very seldom called me up, and I finished my course in a
manner that surprised every one. In the earlier period of my

College life the Faculty never approached me, either to know what my wishes or thoughts were in respect to an appointment, and that course which was deemed judicious at that time was persistently carried out to the end, and when I left town I was allowed to leave without any greater weight than the ordinary sheep-skin which nature and Colleges endow men with.

I went to the far West, and you may suppose I never forgot Amherst. I remember those College days and nights which I spent here. No one searched the sides of the mountains more effectually than I; if there is any one better acquainted with the paths and the ravines of the mountains, I should like to see him; or if any one could tell better where the moss was the greenest, I should like to see him, too. I learned much of Dr. Humphrey, for I saw a man, and after all, the sight of manhood wrought out is better than any theory in a book. His shadow fell upon me, and I have been a braver man and a patient man ever since. I respect him almost as much as I respect my father. I owe a great deal to Dr. Hitchcock; I can not say how much he got from me; I boarded in his family. I had often noticed that when I was talking to him, sometimes he looked very sober—he was thinking about something. I derived much from him, a man most swift of thought and most slow and hesitating of speech. But when his lips gave permission to speak, they were kind words and dropped as gold and silver into the minds of those round about him; I received much from him. I received much from Professor Snell, though he did not believe it. The fact is, I squeezed the honey out of the honeycomb, and left the comb behind.

There was many a morning when the bell rung in the winter for prayers that I did not hear the first bell, and heard the second only in time to shoot into a part of my garments and rush with a cloak into the chapel. But in the summer mornings I

13

often not only heard the first bell ring, but I was in the tower above watching for the sunrise. I have noticed Dr. Storrs talks about the sunsets, but never about the sunrises. I used to sit and see the sun rise, and a more magnificent sight I never knew. I saw and trembled. Like a strong man the sun came forth out of his sleeping tent, while the valley was silvered over with an ocean of fog. He arose higher and higher, shedding his beams gradually around, and illuminating the hills with his glorious rays. I came down from my watch-tower, on those occasions, feeling, I suppose, very much as a bottle of champagne when it is very full of sparkle, but can not get out. Through the mountains, through the vales, through all the things that grow upon them, through all those living things in nature, there are influences which instruct and guide us in the wisdom and power of the Creator. Amherst, to me, has ever been a model college, because, more than Harvard, more than New Haven, perhaps more than Williamstown, —I will not say quite, as it might seem an ungenerous rivalry,— more than almost any other college, God has planted it where man who has eyes to see, and ears to hear, and a mind to instruct, can profit. There is more to be learned outside of its college doors than outside of the doors of any other college in the land.

I am glad that the Trustees, at their latest session, have voted to establish a new professorship in Amherst of history and political economy. This is, until the endowment can be secured to support a full Professor, to be served as best it may be. I think that when it is understood by the friends of Amherst that this professorship is much needed to bring Amherst up to many other colleges, the pleas for an ample endowment will soon be responded to, and before we come here another year, we hope to have the gratifying intelligence that the professorship is established and provided with an able instructor.

The Governor has alluded to another matter which I wish to say one single word about, and that to discriminate rather than to advocate. There has been an application on the part of two young ladies to be admitted to instruction in this College, if they are competent to pass the ordinary examination. That matter is under advisement at present by the Board of Trustees. It is very desirable that vague rumors should not go abroad on this subject, and that the questions now under consideration have no connection with those under the general designation of the woman question or the suffrage question. There is nothing of that kind in connection with this matter. It may pass, or it may not pass. Many of the most advanced thinkers on the subject of woman's rights would see their theories practically tried, but however that may be, we have nothing to do with it. It may be best, or it may not be best that woman should have the right to vote. I for one think it would be for her benefit, but others, wise men and most excellent, are just as positive on the other side. There is no new question proposed. The question whether women shall have the right to the highest education which it is possible to gain in America, has been settled, and that long ago. If there is one thing in which America stands pre-eminent, it is this: We believe that women should be educated according to the measure of her desire and capacity. Unrebuked, women colleges have been established, besides academies and seminaries, and when the question arises as to whether women can have the benefit of a collegiate course, it is met in this way, that we have already more colleges than we have need of. Why should we put two schools to do the work of one? Are women so much like men that they need but one church, one catechism, one minister ; alike in almost everything, and yet so different that they need two sets of instructors, one for men, and one for women in ordinary matters of education? Why, in all the States we are erecting new academies and colleges a hundred years ahead of our pecuniary means. Why should we be doubling the cost of education? Why, if Amherst used the power to instruct these advanced scholars among women, who wish to be teachers and professors, and laborers in the highest fields of science ; if Amherst had the liberality to do it, would it be necessary to put half a million dollars into a woman's school at Northampton, and another five hundred thousand to make it good for anything? This is like a man spending every cent of money in building his factory, and yet without a cent to pay for an engine to run it.

We have plenty of colleges, if only used in a legitimate manner. It is a question of economy. In New England we all understand the worth of an economic article,—it is a "heap sight cheaper" to educate women with men. I know that there are other considerations in the matter. It is said, I am aware, that women do not want it. If they do not, there is no trouble. If the women can not bear the experiences of a collegiate course, then they will go away. This is what men do when they can not sustain it, and by and by, when it is understood that it is not the mere glance of the eye, the exquisite curl, but that life opens to them a fair chance to take on the whole armor of education, the opportunity will be seized upon. I believe it will react on the health of the community. If a woman is strong enough to take care of a baby for eighteen months, and then eighteen months again, and eighteen months afterwards, and then again eighteen months, and then to take care of seventeen children ranging all the way up, with a husband to look after, in addition, with the boys to send to college, and the girls to watch over, she does more than any student can do. There are no nobler spheres than those of the household, but if woman can take care of them, she has got strength enough to get an education. She can stand the college if she can stand the nursery. It is said that it may interfere with the student's attention to studies. It may, but not among the young ladies. No woman will ever undertake a college course unless she has made up her mind to go through. A great many men come here as a mere matter of routine — just because the parental bow shot them here. I like a spirit of fanaticism on this question. I have a son I want to have come here next year. He evidently does not care much about it, but I am bound to have him come. A woman who determines to be highly educated in the sciences and classics should be applauded and helped on.

I know it is settled that women are different from men. Of course they are. I know it is said that they can not do everything that man can do. I do not want them to. If you plant a rose tree and lilacs in the same ground, the plants and flowers will bear their respective flowers and foliage. So from a collegiate course a woman will take that which assimilates with her own nature, and will be a woman still, and not a womanish man. I was brought up in my sister's school at Hartford. That accounts for my womanish ways. But it is all outside, for I am inside, a man. A woman would make a womanish use of this education, and that is what I want to see, a woman's own influence brought to bear in art and literature; it is to make her more woman, and with her power will still be womanly pure. Highly developed in culture her refining influences will be richer and more heavenly.

Amherst is for a universal education. If a man be black, and is fully prepared, or a woman, and is fully qualified, its doors will open to them. Amherst should lead in this march of progress, and if she does, it will not be the first time that she has led in progress and philanthropy. Amherst will do her duty, because she is sent to accomplish a great work, a work which is just and right.

PROF. R. D. HITCHCOCK'S ADDRESS.

Mr. President, and Brethren of the Alumni:—A little more than a year ago, your Historian and I were in Egypt together. We had been up to the First Cataract, and had got back nearly to Cairo. Our boat, the "Ibis," was drifting lazily down the Nile. The Pyramids were in sight again. We were soon to part company, he heading for Rome and I for Sinai. We had engaged to draw up some sort of a Circular for this Amherst Jubilee. It was not an easy thing to do. We had been too long among antiquities that *were* antiquities. Cambyses had come to seem nearer to us than Christopher Columbus used to. With all those "forty centuries" looking down upon us, this little half century of a New England college seemed hardly worth celebrating.

Now that we are back again where nothing is old but the continent itself, half centuries are of some account. At any rate, this one of ours is all we can have at present, and we must make the most of it. In some respects, it is such a half century as the world has never seen before. Indeed, this whole nineteenth century has a very pronounced character; resembling the fifteenth, but going far beyond it, in the same general career of invention and discovery. With improved telescopes, we have reconstructed the Solar System. Our own globe has been probed and peeled by science as one may peel an onion to the core. Steam and electricity have turned things end for

end, and inside out.   Railways are almost everywhere on the
land, and steamboats on the water.   Mountains, deserts, and
seas, which used to be good boundaries, are now but little better than rivers.   Once it required a miracle to make iron swim ;
now it not only swims itself, but floats a good part of the commerce of the world.   Not long ago we waited ten days for our
letters from Liverpool ;   now we get "telegrams," (a new word,
by the by,) ahead of time itself.   With all our fast habits, the
average length of human life is growing steadily greater ;   so
much better care is taken of us by the doctors.   And although
modern life insurance companies can not keep us from dying,
the honestly managed ones, may keep the wolf from the door
when we are gone.

   These things, and the like of these, are what we have been
about now for some time back.   They are not to be despised.
But I think we had better not be too boastful of them.   They
are not the Kingdom of God, by a · great deal.   If they point
that way, it is not of themselves, but of that grand Providence
which overmasters every thing.   Essentially, they are all of one
type—materialistic ;   born of materialism, and breeding materialism.   Something finer than we have yet seen, may come of
them, or in spite of them, by and by ;   must come, if we are
to hold our own.   It was Asiatic wealth which made an end of
the Greeks, and afterwards of the Romans.   It is money that
is hurting us ; money too quickly got, crude, undigested money,
which breaks out in sores upon the body social and politic.
We have been growing rich too rapidly.   Almost every body
seems determined, at all events, not to be poor.   Reputation
itself is getting to be valued for what it will fetch in the market.
This greed of gain is in the air.   Our boys and girls all catch
it.   When we say a man is "well off," we mean that he has a
large income.   If ever a people needed spiritual tonics and an-

tidotes, safeguards, light-houses, anchors, bulwarks, and muni-
tions, we are that people. There is no danger of our being too
often told that man shall not live by bread alone. The common
school may do something for us in stemming this heavy tide; and
the pulpit may do much. But without the higher culture, represented and aimed at by the college, we are certain to go under.

And what do we mean by "college"? I, for one, mean the
old-fashioned American college, which takes boys and *drills*
them, drills them severely, in Latin, Greek, and Mathematics.
Other studies must come in, such as Logic, Metaphysics, Ethics,
History, Political Economy, the Modern Languages, and the
Natural Sciences; but Latin, Greek, and the pure Mathematics
are simply indispensable. There is no such thing as scholarship without them, whatever else there may be. They should
no more be optional studies in college, than reading, writing,
and arithmetic are optional studies in the common school.
Bright boys are none the brighter for being inexact, poor scholars; and dull boys are none the duller for being exact, good
scholars. Well-informed our students ought to be, wide-awake
to what is going on in the world; but the first and the last
necessity, is mental discipline. Without it, the human mind is
not to be trusted. Its action is liable to be as wild as the cuts
and thrusts of a fencer who has never been taught the art of
fencing. That classical and mathematical studies are not practical, is one of the shallowest and most pestilent assertions ever
made. English statesmanship is commonly thought to be rather
practical; and we all know how English statesmen are trained
at Oxford and Cambridge. As for our American statesmanship, its blunders and crudities would certainly be fewer, if only
our statesmen were better scholars. Daniel Webster's genius,
as he said of it himself, was a genius for hard work. I wish
we had more of it, in college and everywhere else.

14

Just now we are trying our hand at universities ; and over-doing the business, I think. "Go to, let us have a university," reminds me of the cry at Babel. Universities, it would be well for us to remember, are not made, they grow. This broader culture, now so much talked of, which has no exact, deep, solid culture underlying it, is a statue without a pedestal, a house upon the sand. Harvard and Yale are rapidly developing into universities, or rather they are becoming universities, as well as colleges. And for New England, these two will be enough. Our other colleges had better stay essentially as they are ; aiming ever higher and higher, to be sure, but always in the same general direction. If already the curriculum is wider, and the standard higher than it was, it is because our academies are better. Much of what is done in college, in Latin, Greek, and the Mathematics, is still altogether too elementary. But till we have more academies like those at Exeter, Andover, and Easthampton, there is really no help for it. The college must take such scholars as it can get, and do the best it may for them. Trained men are what we want, and there is no short and easy way of training them. It is drill, drill, drill, that makes the scholar and the man. Provision may be made for limited and special courses of instruction which exclude the disciplinary studies, but the college proper should remain intact. Nothing should be yielded to the outcry, now so loud, against the dead languages.

We Amherst men are not ashamed of our history so far. Our Alma Mater has now some 1,500 living Alumni, scattered all over the United States, and almost all over the world. Half of these are clergymen, every tenth man of whom is a Foreign Missionary. The other learned professions are of course not so largely represented. We have rather more than a hundred physicians, and nearly twice that number of lawyers. More than two hundred of our Alumni are teachers, a large part of them in institutions of the higher grades. This last item speaks well for the solidity and thoroughness of the training here. With a fair proportion of conspicuous and brilliant men, our graduates, in general, are rather of the plain, sober, and useful type ; enlisted for service, and working or fighting, as the need may be. Their motto might well be :

Dextra tenet calamum, strictum tenet altera ferrum.

A great deal of hard work has been done by our Alumni ; work at the very foundations of Church and State. Nor was courage wanting when the institutions of the country had to be saved by civil war. Nearly two hundred of the sons of Amherst imperilled, and twenty-six of them gave up their lives in the conflict.

So much for the past. To-day we embalm and bury it. Now for the future. What mistakes have been made during the first half century, ought not to be repeated during the next half. And what has been laboriously and wisely settled, should not be unsettled rashly. This College has its own traditions, not to be set aside by anybody. For one thing, its religious and moral tone has made it many friends. Boys have been sent here for moral safety, and have found it. If ever there was any narrowness, or undue pressure, in this regard, provoking resistance, nothing of this sort can be complained of now. This College is as liberal as any other. Many things may be changed as time wears on, but not this capital feature of our history, that this is a Christian College.

We are now exhorted to a "new departure" in admitting women to our classes. I will not debate the question here. But when "golden opportunities" are spoken of, we had better remember,

All that glisters is not gold ;
Often have you heard that told.

I have been requested to say a word about our class scholarships. Two years ago we resolved, if possible, to get a scholarship for every class that has left these halls. The fifty scholarships are not all secured yet, but from present appearances I am sure they will be soon. Some of the earlier classes have been provided for by gentlemen outside of us; Mr. Wells Southworth of New Haven, for example, adopting the class of 1822, and Mr. A. J. Johnson of New York the class of 1823. Who will immortalize himself by adopting Bela B. Edwards's class of 1824? My own class of 1836 is now at work upon its third scholarship, and may possibly have a fourth. Several other classes report their scholarships completed. Some of the later classes, paying by installments, will require more time. But we shall get our fifty scholarships; and fifty years hence we shall have at least fifty more of them. And there is no calculating the good they will do.

But I am taking more than my share of the time, and must make way for others. You and I, Mr. President, were very fortunate in our generation. We had in our class some good scholars, who were likewise right good fellows, besides some good fellows who were not quite so good scholars. And we had a right good time of it all the way through. In our Senior year we were particularly favored. One Professor was all our own. We were the first and the last here in Amherst to admire the flashing of that keen blade, which has since been waving over wider fields. I would not like to be thought revengeful; but I was called up every day or two all that year, and now I must retaliate by calling up our honored instructor of five and thirty years ago, Professor Park of Andover.

PROFESSOR PARK'S ADDRESS.

Mr. President, and Gentlemen of the Alumni :—I certainly did not expect to be called out with such flattering words as those which have been just uttered; and you probably will not expect to hear anything from me,—for I do not think of anything, —worthy of your attention. I love to recall the memories of the Class of '36. It is true that I devoted one summer to the Class of '35, but I devoted an entire year to the Class of '36, and that was the only class to which I did give a full year's instruction; and therefore I am prepared to say that, so far as my personal knowledge extends, the Class of '36 is the worthiest which was ever graduated at the college. In the Historical Address, to which we listened with so much interest this morning, it was implied that the best classes of the college are those which have left it most recently. It is a beautiful statement; but how can it be *proved* that the class of the " Benjamins," is superior to its elder brothers? It is a poetical idea; but we are now inquiring for the sober prose. That address was historical; let us then appeal to history. In the classes which have most recently left the College, where is the learned Judge, the accomplished Governor of Massachusetts, the Doctor of Divinity, the erudite Professor in the Theological Seminary? The Judge, the Governor, the Doctor, the Professor, are in the Class of '36. This is the naked fact.

The careful scholar who instructed us so pleasantly in the

morning, either said or implied, that certain Professors who remained but a short time in the Institution, did not exert a permanent influence upon it.   I am one of those Professors ; and
I challenge Professor Tyler to *prove* that I have exerted no
permanent influence here.   When I left the College I urged the
Trustees to transfer Prof. Fiske to the chair which I vacated,
and to place Prof. Tyler in the chair of Prof Fiske ; and now,
after Prof. Tyler has labored with such eminent success in his
office for thirty-five years, how can he *prove* that I, who first
named him for the office, have exerted no permanent influence
on the Institution ?

He uttered many words of merited enconium on Dr. Stearns,
to whose influence is to be ascribed the erection of some fine
edifices which adorn these grounds.   Now I am able to demonstrate, that after I had refused to accept the Presidency of the
Institution, I was the first man who named Dr. Stearns for the
office ; I visited some of the Trustées and made a journey to
Amherst, for the purpose of recommending his appointment ;
and when I look at these new buildings, one of them so majestic, and one so beautiful, I am moved to exclaim : "They are
the result of my declining to take an office in the College."
How then can it be proved that after having reared these edifices by not coming to the Institution, I have exerted no permanent influence upon it ?

The historian of the morning made various remarks which
started in my mind long trains of recollection.   He said, or
implied, that in the early years of the College not much attention was given to æsthetic culture.   He will admit that this
want of attention must have been the fault of the student.
Thirty-six years ago I stood on the tower of the old chapel in
company with Mr. George Bancroft and Miss Harriet Martineau.   That lady admiring the graceful curvature of the dis-

tant hills, the romantic form of the nearer mountains, the beautiful valley through which is the river, winding at its own sweet will, exclaimed : " This is a school of the Fine Arts." In this school, some men of exquisite taste had been already educated. One of them, Prof. B. B. Edwards, may be fitly named at this hour of our reminiscences. He entered the first Sophomore Class of the College ; was one of the earliest tutors ; was the first Alumnus ever chosen to be a Trustee of the Institution ; he was noted for his delicate sense of the beautiful as well as for the general refinement of his character ; and he often said, that he learned the principles of taste from the woodlands and meadows, the trees and flowers, the hills and groves, which make the scenery of Amherst so instructive, as well as delightful. He once made the remark,—and as I listened to the new chiming bells upon the new chapel-tower this morning, I recalled his almost prophetic utterance—that " nothing would become Amherst so well as a chime of bells, and no place would be so appropriate for a chime of bells as a tower of Amherst College." He did not live to experience the realization of his dream ; but no one would rejoice more than he, to notice that art is now adding her charms to those of nature, and both are combining to make this scene the joy of the whole earth.

Miss Martineau, as she surveyed the grounds nearest the chapel, remarked that " time would be necessary to give them the grace and finish which belong to Oxford, Cambridge, and other of the English schools." But that time is coming. The men who will stand here at the next Semi-centennial will see velvet lawns and serpentine walks around these buildings ; and it will be said of Amherst, as it has been said of Addison's walk in Oxford : " No one treading these grounds can avoid being a poet." At the Centennial celebration of the College, when the princely benefactor of this Institution, the friend in the hour of its need, shall have been numbered with his fathers, a statue of bronze will be raised to his honor among the venerable trees which will then shade these walks ; for he is the man who, in the first place, had the enterprise and the industry to amass a fortune ; in the second place, had the prudence and the sagacity to keep a fortune ; in the third place, had the patriotism and the philanthropy to give a fortune away. An Alumnus of this Institution, in a recent speech at the unveiling of Washington Irving's statue in New York, said that similar statues would be erected to ministers of the Gospel, if the time should ever come when any of them would be both good and handsome. At the next Semi-centennial, numerous marble busts of the Alumni will adorn these halls ; and among them will be seen a life-like statue of the Alumnus who uttered that prophecy ; for he has the three titles to the honor ; he is a clergyman, and good, and handsome ; and men will love to gaze at the image of the man who has just described to us the manner of his studying the mathematics with Professor Snell.

It is not, however, by its aesthetic culture, that Amherst has been chiefly distinguished ; it is by its hard work. At the present day there are great improvements in the method of education ; but there can be no improvement which will dispense with the personal toil of the pupil. Some usages of the schools have become antiquated ; but severe labor can never go out of date. Even a poet who is born, not made, must superadd industry to his inheritance, or he is born to " waste his sweetness on the desert air." I remember an incident which occurred at the commencement of this College, thirty-six years ago ; and I now allude to it as illustrating the fact, that no kind of excellence is attained without care. Mr. Edward Everett was delivering the Oration before the Literary Societies. Near the close of his Oration, he uttered the following sentence : " Be-

fore the admiring student of nature has realized all the won-
ders of the elder world, thus, as it were, re-created by science, another delightful instructress, with her microscope in
her hand, bids him sit down and learn at last to know the universe in which he lives ; and contemplate the limbs, the mo-
tions, the circulations of races of animals, disporting in *their*
tempestuous ocean,—*a drop of water*." I have now read the
sentence ; you have listened to it without excitement ; you still
appear to be calm and serene. But when it was uttered by
Mr. Everett, the audience was convulsed with emotion. Young
men and old men were moved with wonder as well as delight.
What was the secret of this power ? The secret lay in the
naturalness of Mr. Everett's thoroughly studied elocution ; in
the artlessness of his rhetorical art. As he uttered those memorable words, "*a drop of water*," he turned around ; saw, as if
for the first time, a glass of water on the table at his side ; he
put his finger into the glass, as if the thought of doing so had
just occurred to him ; he raised his finger with the drop of
water suspended from it ; we gazed at the drop ; it was a globe,
teeming with inhabitants ; the globe fell upon the platform ;
and while those myriads of inhabitants, as good by nature as
ourselves, were taking their last gasp, the spectators, lettered
and unlettered, laymen and divines, were tumultuous in their
applause. We all supposed that this dramatic elocution was un-
premeditated. I have since heard that several weeks before
the oration was delivered, the pains-taking author of it wrote
a letter, inquiring whether it would be proper to introduce such
an unusual gesture in an address to such an audience as that of
the literati of Amherst College. The effectiveness of that one
sentence explains the fact that as mere *readers*, we can form no
conception of the power which was felt by the *hearers*, of the
great speeches uttered by the Grecian and Roman orators. I

15

do not mean to imply that I approve, for I do not approve, of such excessive solicitude about the *minutiæ* of oratory ; but I believe in the lesson which it suggests, and which has been the first, second and third lesson taught in this college, that all eloquence, and all kinds of excellence, even the poetical, are the result of industry. It is the industry of the Alumni of Amherst which has made them marked men in all parts of the globe. The fruits of their toil are seen in the Christian Missions of Asia and Africa. Much has been said this afternoon in regard to the education of women. I think that the graduates of Amherst, so many of whom have been distinguished for practical sense, have done a signal work in advancing this education. I do not believe that the Mount Holyoke Seminary,—and that is a school which has exerted a healthful influence in behalf of woman's rights—would have ever been what it is now, had it not received the efficient aid of President Hitchcock, Prof. Tyler, Prof. B. B. Edwards, and other Alumni and officers of this Institution. I must think that the college which has been recently endowed by Miss Sophia Smith, and which is soon to grace the already beautiful town of Northampton, will contribute much to the true honor of women, and will make hundreds of them, without the aid of the Supreme Court of Massachusetts, real Justices of the Peace. But that college would probably never have been devised, had it not been for an Alumnus of this Institution. He was laboring peacefully in one of the charming villages on the banks of the Connecticut ; and there, in his modest and quiet way, he set in motion a train of influences which will soon give a new college, and an attractive ornament to the State of Massachusetts. I have been looking around this audience in the hope of seeing that real working man here ; but I do not detect him. If I knew that he was present, I would call his name. I will not expose an absent man, however; and will only say that, although I have praised my own humility,—and there is no virtue of which I am so proud as I am of my humility,—in declining an office in Amherst. College, and thus erecting these costly buildings, yet, long after my name shall have faded away and dropped like a sere and yellow leaf from the remembrance of men, the name of that man will still be Green.

I shall not speak on the question which has been proposed this afternoon in regard to admitting women into the regular classes of your Alma Mater; but as this is the time for college reminiscences, I will repeat a saying of President Humphrey, who has been fitly extolled this afternoon as a wise and sound man. There was one student connected with the Institution who neglected his studies,—I must presume there was only one,—and, at a meeting of the Faculty, there was a prolonged discussion in regard to the cause of his remissness. One Professor thought that the young man was troubled with the headache; another thought that he had a fever; still another thought that he was burdened with pecuniary embarrassment. At length the President uttered, with a pause after almost every syllable, these suggestive words: "I have reason to believe that the remissness of the young man is owing to a shock which he has received from a *gal*—vanic battery."

SPEECH OF WALDO HUTCHINS, ESQ.

Mr. President, and my Brother Alumni :—I understand I am
to do justice to the occasion, because I was so fortunate as to
marry one of Dr. Webster's grand-daughters.   Now, under the
circumstances of this case, I am inclined to follow very much
the resolution which I noticed recently introduced into the
Nebraska constitutional convention, by one of its most able
members, providing that hereafter women shall take the place
of men in all the occupations of life, and that the word "male"
shall be stricken out of the constitution, and "female" inserted.
I must say that I fully agree in this proposition, but I am sorry
to be compelled to add that my wife, with whom I have just had
conference, tells me that in her day, Amherst College did not
permit women to be educated within its walls—that she does
not feel competent to speak upon this occasion, and calls upon
me to be her substitute.   She wishes me to add that at the
centennial anniversary she hopes that her great-great-grand-
daughter may be permitted to make an address upon that occasion.   I suppose you all know where I stand on this question.   I suppose you will throw me on the side of opening the
doors wide open for all who desire to come within its walls, and
receive the best education that can be obtained.

But I am expected to say something of Noah Webster, and
of his early connection with this college.   He came here in
1812, and at that time there was no school of a higher grade

than the common district school held in a small room, where the boys and girls were educated together. That was the school Amherst enjoyed in that day. He came here with a mind seeking more leisure to follow his favorite pursuit, and live with greater economy, having a large family dependent upon him for support. After a while the educated men of this vicinity met in his parlor for consultation upon the educational interest of this section of the country, and the result was the establishment of Amherst academy, which proved a great success. About that time the question was agitated of the removal of Williams College. It was considered by many friends of education to be in a too remote section of the State, and it was believed that the interests of education would be greatly subserved by its removal to a more central location. Dr. Webster went into it with all the ardor and zeal characteristic of him. He believed that Williams College would be better if removed to the center of the State. But we have reason to bless God that this agitation of the subject, although it did not result in the removal of Williams College, was the means of establishing Amherst College.

I hold in my hands a passage of three or four lines, which strikingly illustrates the anxiety of our ancestors in the matter of education : "After God had carried us safe to New England, and we had builded our homes, provided the means of livelihood for our families, reared a convenient place for God's worship, and settled civil government, one of the next things we long for and look for is to advance learning and to perpetuate it to posterity, dreading to leave an illiterate ministry to the churches when our present ministry shall be in the dust." It was the spirit of this noble sentiment that governed Dr. Webster and actuated him in giving his services with those other noble men who founded Amherst College. Could he have been spared to be with us to-day, and see these noble buildings, these monuments of Christian liberality and philanthropy, how' would his heart throb with joy, and what an earnest prayer of thankfulness would he send up to the Giver of all good gifts. I remember in the fall of 1841 he attended college prayers one evening in company with President Humphrey, and made a few remarks to the students. I can recall distinctly, as though it were to-day, his erect and dignified form. With solemn voice, tremulous with age and emotion, he gave utterance to his thoughts. He spoke of this college, of the necessities which brought it into being, of the interest he had taken in watching over its growth, of its struggles in its infancy, and of his firm belief in its continued growth and prosperity. As he stood there in the autumn twilight he seemed like the patriarch and prophet of old, giving us his parting benediction.

If republican principles are to be fostered, if the people are to be distinguished by their love of intelligence, order and religion, then must we see to it that their nurseries of learning planted upon the hill-tops and in the valleys of our country are liberally, yea, generously supported. Why, imagine if you can for one moment all our colleges and all our educational institutions blotted out? What a strangeness would come over the land and what a feeling of despair would seize upon the people. As long as we know of their existence and feel their beneficial influence, we experience the same feeling of safety and of relief as does the midnight mariner when amidst the darkness and the storm he sees afar out across the waste of waters the beacon light which warns him of the dangers that lie in his pathway, and which guide him to the haven of safety.

Somewhat more than a year ago to-day I was in the old city of Mecklenburg, in Prussia, and while there I passed the cathedral, one of the noble Gothic edifices in Northern Germany.

I heard the sound of music within its walls. I went in, and there I saw arrayed in martial line and order thousands of young Prussian soldiers, each of them bearing an earnest, intelligent and honest countenance. As the organ pealed forth, accompanied by a full choir of manly voices, these young soldiers advanced, column by column, to the altar, and there received, in a solemn and reverential manner, the sacrament of the Lord's Supper. Six weeks later, I was in the French city of Strasbourg, on the day on which war was declared by France against Prussia. I saw there thousands of French soldiers, martial-looking men, eager for the fray, breathing vengeance against Prussia, and jubilant in the idea of speedy victory. I saw on one side, an intelligent and God-fearing people ; upon the other side, an uneducated, self-reliant soldier, and could the result be doubtful? Was it not what would have been expected? Intelligence, virtue and education behind the needle-gun ; ignorance, infidelity and sensuality behind the chassepot. Prussia to-day takes rank among the foremost nations of Europe, and France, with all her traditional glory, all her love of country, sinks to the position of a second-rate power. Her loss of prestige to-day, will inure to her greatness and glory in the future.

Let those who are building up the republic see to it that it is built upon intelligence, virtue and religion, the only sure and safe guaranties for a free and happy republic.

PROF. H. B. HACKETT'S ADDRESS.

I FEEL, Mr. President, that I might justly ask to be excused from attempting to say anything on this occasion, certainly as a representative of the class of 1830; for this class has been amply and admirably represented by the orator and historian to whom we listened in the forenoon.   For myself, I am proud as a member of the class of 1830, to claim him as one of our number.   It is not every Professor who understands Greek, that understands English as well.   We who knew Professor Tyler at the beginning, are not surprised at such versatility in him.   The discourse which we heard from him, so elaborate, instructive, and eloquent, simply shows that as he began, so he has gone on, nobly fulfilling the bright promise of his college days.

Goldsmith used to say that when at the university he made but a poor a figure in the mathematics, but could turn an ode of Homer into English equal to the best of them.   Our Tyler was good in everything; he could produce a sensation in conic sections, or the calculus, as well as in Horace or Homer.   He learned to good purpose in those days the old poet's dictum, as good for actual life as for the mimic stage,—

> "Ad imum
> Qualis ab incepto processerit et sibi constet."

The learned orator, therefore, stands before us to-day justly crowned with the laurels which he wears.   I hope the heresy, rebuked by such an example, that dull and idle boys make the smartest men, will never find its way into Amherst College.

The older brothers of the College rejoice most heartily with their younger brothers in the manifold prosperity of the College as we see it to-day, at the end of these first fifty years. But as I listened to the orator's account of the difficulties and trials which the friends and first teachers of the College had to encounter forty years ago,—the period of my connection with it,—I felt that I might justly characterize that period, at least, as the *heroic* age in the history of the College. The age is heroic that produces heroic men ; and it was these early trials of courage, faith, disinterestedness, which gave us such characters as those of HEMAN HUMPHREY, EDWARD HITCHCOCK, NATHAN W. FISKE, and others. I account it one of my greatest obligations to the College, that it gave me the benefit of the example and the teachings of such men. I can truthfully say that my remembrance of their disinterestedness, fidelity and self-denial has ever been among the best inspirations of my life.

I have followed the history of my class-mates—about forty of us—with some care. Several of them, of whose usefulness and success we had reason to entertain the best hopes, died early. The one of these first taken was the youngest of our number. We who knew them, have not forgotten them. We linger longest at the graves, in which have been buried "the hopes of unaccomplished years." Of the rest, I know enough to say that they have all been in their various spheres upright, earnest, useful men. No one of them has yet dishonored the College, or brought a stain upon his own personal reputation. Four of them have been missionaries of the cross in foreign lands. Schneider discoursed to us at our commencement, (possibly the Junior exhibition) on the *felicity* of *benevolence,* and having now tried his theory for nearly forty years, still lives to

16

testify by word and deed that the way to be happy is to be unselfish. The record of his labors and successes in Asia Minor
reads like a page from the Acts of the Apostles.

It is a cause of regret to me—I feel it keenly to-day—that I
have been since my graduation so seldom present at the commencements of the College. I have been leading all this time
since I left here, a somewhat vagrant, academic life. During
all these years, I have been, without a single year's exception,
cooped up within college walls, either as a pupil in professional
schools, or as a teacher in colleges and seminaries. I have
thus formed, of course, new literary attachments and responsibilities, more or less engrossing; but I can truly say, as I come
back again to-day from these wanderings to the old *Alma Mater*
—for *old* assuredly she must be, when so many sons rise up with
hoary heads to do her homage—I can truly say to-day to this
dear mother of us all :

"My heart untraveled fondly turns to thee."

Of this I am confident. No one can rejoice more heartily
than I do, in the bright auguries which introduce this second
Semi-centennial of Amherst College.

SPEECH OF BISHOP HUNTINGTON.

WHERE the family circle is so full, Mr. President, and where every mother's son has the same claim to be heard, we must go as directly as we can to the principal matters in mind.

Among the honorable points in the history of this College, I am struck first with this. It is a natural product of the soil that supports it. Standing in the very heart of New England, it owns and represents its place. Its life is New England life, through and through. From the first breath of its infancy, fifty years ago, it has never tasted a whiff of any other than New England air. Rooted in this Massachusetts earth, between the ledges of rocky hills and the alluvial river-meadows, the mingled Puritanic strength and philanthropic sweetness of the juices of the mountain and the valley seem to have gone into its blood. It is not a transplanted stock. Not an exotic hue or outlandish feature can be seen on its face. Its energies, endurance, successes, its *ethos*, as an Athenian might say, its virtue, as we, its children, may certainly say, and its blemishes, if it has them, belong to the ground that has grown it, and the climate that has ripened it. If foreign ideas have ever arrived and dismounted at this door, it has fared with them a good deal as it did with the polite and amiable French master that came, in the summer of '36, to teach our class, when we were sophomores, the French pronunciation. There were two windows, and they always happened to be open, on the north side of the recitation room, and from the moment the roll was called a silent process of waste began on that end of the seats, till, somehow, when the hour was up, through the doorway, along with the unobservant and smiling tutor, only

Three "angels issued where " threescore " went in."

After the war with England was over, the thrifty farmers, the prosperous traders and the orthodox ministers in this part of the country, wanted a college to train their sons, not quite so far west as Williams, and not quite so far toward Plato as Cambridge. Without many educational theories or much noise they arose and built, somewhat as their Hebrew prototypes did, building with one hand, while they held not a sword or spear, exactly, but the plow or the pruning-hook, into which Peace had beaten them, with the other, "from the rising of the morning till the stars appeared." He that "sounded the trumpet," too, was by them. It was not the trumpet of their own liberality or destiny, —American ears have since become more familiar with these notes,—but of the promises of God to patient toil. Thus Amherst College had its legitimate birth and beginning. It was not so much a manufacture after a pattern as a growth out of a vital seed. Its fathers and its sons were *autochthonoi*,—children of the land. The New England tree yielded after its kind. The common mind, by the operation of a common sense, created it, but with uncommon forecast and resolution. The State was slow to help it, but the people had their way, because they made the way. It was set as a crown on this hill-top, in the midst of a beauty as bright and fair as any that the beauty-loving eyes of Greek students could find between Mounts Athos and Olympus. It came to be what it is,—a kind of indigenous republican Acropolis of letters,—a living, literary and religious power.

Natural beginnings do not always insure a worthy career. It

seems to me to be another of the fine characters marking this history, that the institution has followed the laws of honest health in its half century of practical progress. As it was not fashioned by programme or pet scheme, it has been the victim of no educational speculation or sentimental hobby-rider at any period. Look at the list of its presidents, not long, to be sure, but clean and estimable. Neither they nor its professors, least of all its trustees, have been visionary persons, ambitious of sudden celebrity, blowers of bubbles, casters-up of short roads or royal roads, or over-broad roads to learning. It is something to say of any seminary in these loud times, that it never solicited patronage on self-assertion, or relied on other certificates than the men it moulded. In the morbid modern appetite for new measures, it seems sometimes to be a positive recommendation to confidence in a thing, that it was never heard of before. I can think of no one of these faithful instructors and disciplinarians, from the first, who has coveted any factitious distinction, who has made a sham of his chair, or who has not put his best strength conscientiously into the doing of his term's labor. I think all of them would heartily indorse that definition of genius which calls it a transcendent capacity for taking pains. One of them, that modest mathematician yonder, quiet and accurate watcher of the clock-work of earth and sky for half a hundred years, who has been at once the contemporary and the benefactor of everything that the college ever was or did, and who, if anybody, is the real living hero of this day, never, I warrant you, had a night's sleep hurt by dreams of revolutionizing the diagram of the heavens or reconstructing the weather. They that become prophets and priests of nature do not patronize her, but sit at her feet. It is a part of the vocation of our thorough-bred students to correct, if they can, the popular impatience for immediate results; to show this eager age that

mere "dash" without drill is a dash into rout and ruin; and
that, while the maxim of "head-quarters in the saddle and no
base of supplies" may do well enough for sham fighters at a
village muster, it will never make very short work of our long
war with ignorance and error.   But there are qualities of a different order.   These teachers of ours, we all know, have not
been in bondage to the old any more than wild adventurers after the new.   Staying at their posts, in the several departments,
whatever light has glimmered anywhere, through archæology or
invention, they have welcomed.   Under this wakeful regimen,
the standard of scholarship has been constantly rising; the curriculum has been enlarged; the intellectual supply has been
deeper and wider all the while.   Apparatus, cabinets, two of
them not surpassed in any of the universities, the buildings, the
examination papers, the commencements, tell their own story
better than our laudatory tongues can tell it.   The College has
kept itself in quick sympathy with .the pulse of the people, in
the national agonies and sacrifices, in war and peace, in the
general instincts of patriotism, in the interests of industry and
charity.   I remember one of the college halls was thrown open
once for a cattle-show address before the county agricultural
society.   The martyr scroll of fallen soldiers shines as splen-
didly before your eyes to-day as the early heroism of Greece
did in the eloquence and marble of its Attic orators and later
sculptors.   Would these new structures, so solid and costly,
have ever been reared, if the givers, men of business and calcu-
lation, had not been sure that there was a cordial response in
this staff of scholars to every genuine impulse of humanity in
the community around it?   They are the visible answer, as
I take it, uttered in stone and iron, of earnestness in the men
of action to earnestness in the men of thought.   Thought and
action have been finding out that they are not alien forces, not

jealous competitors, but that each is strong and free only as it acknowledges its brother, and as both move side by side. A conviction of this deep-seated concord is wrought, it seems to me, into the whole cultus and spirit of this nursery of thinking brains and manly men. Most of all ought we to render unceasing homage to these teachers, for a lesson as grand as any in the books. In the dark days of an exhausted treasury, complete poverty and threatened death, with a self-denial as uncomplaining as it was unassuming, they took up the burden of unrequited labor, ran the bold venture of a livelihood without a salary, and by going half way to starvation, saved the cause. None of us can feel a relish so keen as theirs in the joy of this jubilee. The success that we are witnessing, then, is not a trick or an accident. It has been honestly earned.

Hitherto, in most American colleges, the idea of moral discipline under academic law has been united with that of the impartation of knowledge and the training of the intellectual powers. A legal regulation and restraint have been considered indispensable to the teaching function and the order of the collegiate community. Undergraduates have been held as boys rather than men. Their immaturity has subjected them to a government of specific, local rules The administration of an authority like that, lying in an undefined region between the family, where love is more than law, and the civil court, where law is more than love, proves, as everybody who has tried it knows, to be one of exceeding delicacy and perplexity. Periodical rebellions and chronic irritations have abundantly illustrated the difficulty. Weak sympathies in unreasonable parents, on the one side, and official vanity or arbitrary passion in college officers on the other, complicate it still further. All this is changing. An advance of studies carries forward the average age of the members of the classes. The university plan being approximated more and more, self-respect and self-direction take the place of coercion. The students are supposed to be gentlemen, who, if they are matriculated at all, remain for the elected purpose of taking advantage of the instruction, with some inbred scholarly principles. Down to this period, however, every class graduated here has been four years subject to a faculty law. What is the record? Having been born myself two years before the college was, and the spot I always call home lying only a league away from it, I take leave to say,—naming it as our third point of honor,—that this vexing discipline has been conducted, not for any little quadrennial epoch merely, but all along, with even wisdom and singular fidelity. I am not speaking of that dry kind of success which barely succeeds in keeping the peace, or in holding a sullen discontent under suppression and calling it peace. That is the barren regularity of a scene half prison-house and half grave-yard, not the rich, sweet order of a harvest field, where a life of affection·leaps in every intellectual pore and organ. I mean much more than that. I believe it has been the uniform feeling of the administrators of this great trust, that every youth coming or sent here, had not only a mind to be stocked and a memory to be quickened, but a forming manhood to be made pure, vigorous and firm. I believe that very few of these alumni have been able to retain a fair doubt that their instructors were their personal friends, sincerely seeking their highest good. I believe no class ever took its degrees without an almost universal sense of gratitude and esteem for its temporary masters. There has been occasional friction, but as little of it as the nature of the case, human nature, and college nature allow. Rebellion songs, sung out or muttered, have not entered much into the music of our march. Whether the intellectual stimulus of high heads and the contagion of superb scholarship have always acted on the student's enthusiasm or not, he has known himself to be in hands wise and true. So much of the temper of Dr. Arnold of Rugby has, on the whole prevailed, that even the culprit, stung with a sense of being misunderstood and over-punished, has not finally questioned the right conscience and Godward mind of his punisher. Whatever benefits may be expected hereafter to accompany the substitution of self-control for supervision and obedience, there must be a real loss in the severance of these generous and wholesome relations of confidence and loyalty. Character is forever the commanding and comprehensive fact among men. Life is the end as well as the test of learning. And, therefore, there never will be, I hope, as I think there never has been, a time when a young man will be taken in and dealt with here under the horrible imposture that he is a piece of mental mechanism, or a lucrative tributary to the college revenue, or reputation, and not a son of the Lord Almighty,—a spiritual creature to whom the Infinite Spirit has given understanding.

So we are brought, Mr President, to our last and loftiest challenge of the public good-will, growing out of our half-century's history. The college has not subordinated faith to knowledge, or sacrificed knowledge,—absurd immolation!—to faith. It has not committed itself to either one of those destructive falsehoods, that revelation has anything to fear from *thorough* science, or that science can ultimate and complete itself without revelation. Here, my brothers, you may perhaps think it not unfit if I speak with the more emphasis than most of you would, for the very reason of my standing, in a manner, separate from the particular religious system that prevails with you. That question is not at issue now. This institution was founded, has lived, grown and borne fruit, in the faith of Christ, the head of the race and lord of the kingdom of the mind Nay, it has lived, very largely, for the express purpose of extending that

17

faith, by educated preachers and missionaries, training them, as
the mother of Chrysostom said she trained her son, to conquer
a classical heathenism by the weapons of classical learning.   If
it has any clearer title to consideration among civilized men,
seeing on what Corner-stone all civilization rests, or one deserv-
ing to be more celebrated at this celebration, I, for one, do not
know what it is.   No personal distinction has given Amherst a
wider or better fame than that of our distinguished geologist
and naturalist, Professor and President Hitchcock, who has vin-
dicated the harmony between the verities in the structure of the
globe and the verities of the Bible.   Whether it shall finally
turn out that his methods are those on which Christian schools
will mostly rely or not, may be questionable; but that they contain enough of both fact and logic to refute all that has been
brought to disturb that harmony, it is quite safe to say.   Materialism, in the new French and English school, is not by any
means the last word of science on that subject, nor is positive-
ism a new word in the history of negations.   Mr. Farrar has
shown in his Bampton lectures, that there is a manifest recur-
rence in the various shapes of unbelief, and that, in kind, all the
modern forms of neology came into being in the primitive age,
where they were met and broken by the apologists of the primitive church.   There is a reassuring and comforting effect, sug-
gesting that the objections are limited, from that periodicity in
the movements of doubt, but more still in this simple, undenia-
ble proposition; that if science means to be thorough it must
take all the states and conditions of men's experience into its
purview as matters of fact, explaining them and disposing of
them, and the moment it does that, it confronts a spiritual nature with spiritual phenomena,—a whole class of facts which no
philosophy has as yet so much as pretended to account and pro-
vide for independently of religion.   Half-knowledge is at pres-

ent the adversary,—the prolific breeder of self-conceit and so of denials of the faith *once for all* delivered. God in nature and God in the Book is one God. We have only to know better both nature and the Book, by the help of Christian colleges like this, to see and confess it, with joyful adoration, and to find the battle with Atheism, and with its less audacious and less consistent sister-witch, Pantheism, growing lighter. Forward, then, brethren, let us say to ourselves, and to one another!

If the college has not a roll-call of many generations, so much the larger share of its responsible life is in the future; and of that future we are among the builders. Let this stir and sober us. What is there to bar the way against a steady expansion yet to come, as healthful and irresistible as that which has been, till, call it university or not, all that makes up the substantial education of the nineteenth century man, before the century itself is done, shall be here combined and organized? Our traditions may be slight: but our business is to take care what traditions we help make for those that come after us, by large thought, reverent manners, noble living. In the Divine Commonwealth the fiftieth year was one of liberation and Sabbatic rest. One prayer is rising for our Alma Mater, I am sure, from all hearts, in this re-gathering, that she may have long life in the liberty of Christ and in the peace of a heavenly law; that her sons may be a brotherhood of scholars, thinkers, believers, workmen with a wide look and ready hand reaching towards this world's service, and yet ever bending humbly before God, as if nature herself were a sanctuary, learning were a kind of litany, life were worship, and the Savior's cross an inspiring signal never out of their sight.

SPEECH OF HENRY STOCKBRIDGE, ESQ.

Mr. President:—I join most heartily in the congratulations that are befitting an anniversary like this. I congratulate the Trustees, the Faculty, the Alumni, all the friends of this beloved Institution, whether gathered here to-day or detained elsewhere. Nor are my felicitations upon that which happeneth unto all— the noble and the ignoble alike, the *mere* flight of time. If that were all and there was no grateful record of worthy accomplishment to which to point, the occasion were one for humiliation, and condolence only.

But such is not our case. Whether we regard the growth of our Alma Mater as an institution of learning,—the progress made, and the power acquired ; or, the honorable positions attained by her Alumni, and the blessings carried to the world by the brave, manly work which they have done, there is much for which we are called upon to thank God, and from which we may take courage.

To the record of the past of the Institution we have listened as it has been read to us by our chosen·chronicler. To that record I shall not presume to attempt to add a line. Its present he can see, who, having eyes, looks around to-day. Its future is known only to Him who, from the beginning sees the end ; and whatever of cherished hopes or aspirations we may express, it is not folly to heed the admonition of the great humorist:

" Don't never prophesy unless yo *know.*"

That unknown future we are called upon in courage, built on faith, to meet as may become men; to prepare for it as if we could command destiny ; and to act in the earnest belief that

> "The fault is not in our stars
> But in ourselves, *if* we are underlings."

It is this great problem,—the future of our Alma Mater—which this occasion naturally suggests, and to which all our thoughts are drawn. *Here*, perhaps, to some extent, may have arisen the contest which is wider than our country, and as old at least as the days of Rehoboam, between the spirit of change and that of conservatism ; and the clamor of the new for the place occupied by the old, if it has not already entered, can not long be excluded from these halls.

It is true that the interests and guidance of the Institution have been confided to some of our most honored Alumni, and others, their worthy compeers, who had acquired good repute for wisdom before they were called to assume this charge, and who have been enriched by wide observation, and large experience since ; but it would be modesty without precedent elsewhere if *we* did not assume that Alumni, in mass meeting assembled, could instruct their ignorance ; it would be strange if we could forget that though age and experience do not always bring wisdom, youth and inexperience always do ; and our earlier would sadly shame our more advanced (not to say our more mature) years. if having, as undergraduates, guided and managed the Faculty, we can not, as Alumni, guide and manage the Trustees.

We are not officious then, when, gathering from our wide dispersions, and turning from the varied avocations which engross our years, we supplement *their* crude projects with the treasures of our well-considered suggestions ; and we say to them, as was so often said to us,—adapting to the Institution's future the maxim given for personal guidance,—the first grand prerequisite of success is a distinct and definite purpose and aim.

In modern times—for person or institution—the Abrahamic journey, with an a quo, but no ad quem, is a very long one.

The great thought to which Alumni rise so easily, but which is such a stone of stumbling to Trustees, is, ALL KNOWLEDGE FOR ALL HUMANITY. All that is asked of Trustees is the trifling task of providing ways and means, of devising in detail, and putting in working order the machinery which shall effect this result. In other words, we, with every American college, would be a grand university; not on the English plan, where a convention of colleges and halls, with curricula each substantially a copy of the other, united by a corporate bond, constitutes a university, but on the grander plan of the American popular idea of a university, to wit: an institution where the broadest foundation of general, classical and mathematical culture shall be crowned with the most accurate and detailed specialistic and professional trainings, and the graduate comes forth a Minerva in pedigree and equipment, an Apollo in grace

It is easy enough to order a school of general culture which shall be a foundation for all professional pursuits It is easy enough to order a professional school which shall furnish special training for any profession. The ordering of a course of study which shall furnish fit preparation for every profession, and every scientific and artistic pursuit, and at the same time relieve the votary of any one from a waste of labor and of time upon those things which are peculiar to any other, is a problem not quite so easy of solution. Yet this is the problem for the solution of which there is no little popular demand.

Some of us are not prepared to admit that the boys of to-day can make very much larger acquisition by dint of hard work in

a course of four years than was made by some of the boys
a quarter or half a century ago. Nor do we feel certain that
any very valuable discipline or attainment can be poured into
the mind through any funnel yet invented.

If it be true then that the world's work is to be done by
specialists, and the college of the future is to be the nursery in
which they shall be reared, it must be that the college change
its form, or rather, that colleges cluster, not with parallel courses
of study, but with aims clearly differing and defined, and courses
entirely distinct; that round the nucleus of our Alma Mater,
with its literary, humanizing influences, shall gather the schools
of real, practical professional work (of which cluster the noble
institutions already planted on its right by the good old Commonwealth of Massachusetts is but the avant-courier, the first-
born of the coming brotherhood) and that this cluster shall be
made to work harmoniously, each in its allotted sphere, under a
common supervision.

To carry on a work of such magnitude, a munificence of endowment is required such as we have yet hardly ventured to
imagine. Yale, the object in the past of so many rich benefactions, has through one of her most ardent friends, just announced her present pressing, imperative need of eight hundred
thousand dollars to enable her to meet the demands made upon
her to-day.

The accumulations here are yet less than there; the demands now are quite as great, and with every step of progress
the vista widens.

It is unjust as it is idle to join in these demands, or to encourage them, unless we are ready in some manner to contribute substantial aid and comfort to those who bear the burden of
supplying the demand. We have no right to add to their burden, already a most oppressive and embarrassing one, while we

ourselves will not touch it with one of our fingers; to do that, for example, which shall render necessary a professorship of Platonic affections, with the material changes necessarily connected therewith, and yet furnish the institution no new or additional resources.   Too many adherent parasites may exhaust the vitality of the parent stock and draw it, with them, to a common death.

But we are not prophets of evil.   Proud of the past, we are hopeful and confident of the future.   As our Alma Mater in the past has been equal to all the reasonable demands and wise requirements of the times, so may her future be.   For her, though not for us, there is a fountain of youth, and we can not doubt that she will continue to furnish what the world most urgently needs, if not what it most clamorously asks for.   With clustering colleges under a common head, or with varied departments known together as one college, here shall be the home of the broadest, and most thorough classical liberal culture, and the most accurate special training for all practical life; the home at once of catholicity and speciality, a school which the world can not afford to let die; so that when another fifty years is told, they who gather to celebrate its centennial anniversary, whether many or few, and whether the list of names upon its catalogue is long or short, may congratulate each other and proudly boast to the world that it has ever been the school of Christian gentlemen.

SPEECH OF WILLARD MERRILL, ESQ.

Mr. President and Brethren of the Alumni:—I want to give you an extract from Cæsar's commentaries. I would give it to you in the original, but I fear my Latin would be lame, and I am confident the most of you would not understand it whether lame or not. I am equally afraid my translation would be open to criticism should I attempt one, so I will give you the substance of a passage, as I recollect it.

All Gaul is divided into three parts and is inhabited by three different tribes, of which the most rude and barbarous are those who live farthest from the civilization and refinement of our province.

There is a tradition in New England, cherished most by those who have been least away from the old homestead, that of the various parts into which this broad land of ours is divided, the most rude and barbarous are those that are farthest from the civilization and refinement of New England, and under the inspiration of this tradition they are accustomed to regard the North-West as a wild, uncultivated waste, and its inhabitants as a rude, unlettered, migratory and gassy people, with their chief boast and their chief encampment—*Chicago!* And a very learned Doctor of Divinity to illustrate what he considered the migratory and boastful character of a portion of this people, recently said in a public place and to a large audience, that in his travels in Europe he met more people from Illinois than from

18

any other portion of the country, and in every instance upon
the ends of their trunks was Illinois, and on the ends of their
tongues was—*Chicago!*

But, brethren of the Alumni, we meet here to-day as children
of a common Alma Mater, a widely scattered brotherhood. I
trust we are united as one man in our zeal for the fair fame and
continued prosperity of Amherst College. When the honored
President of the College, and the distinguished Professor of
Mental Philosophy, in the fall of 1869, came to the meeting
of the Amherst Alumni of the North-West at Chicago, and
when in the fall of 1870, we were visited in the same place by
that distinguished and venerable man, whom we all love to
honor, Professor Snell, I believe that at our annual festival in
honor of Alma Mater, they found men as loyal and earnest in
their devotion to learning and religion, as can be found in New
England.   And why not?   During the formative period of our
lives we all received the impress of the same kindly, elevating
and inspiriting influences; the same Alma Mater with a steady
hand, checked, guided and controlled us all; the same zeal for
sound learning and thorough discipline, and the same Christian
spirit at all times controlled the Faculty and were thrown about
and infused within the students.

And here I wish to enter my protest against a notion somewhat prevalent at the present day, and which many suppose to
exist, particularly at the North-West. It is said that many of
our colleges devote too much time to the study of the ancient
languages and mathematics and too little to science. It is
claimed that the young man graduating from college should
have his mind richly stored with the facts that will meet him in
practical life.   To this I have no objection, so far as knowledge
is the result of a course of study involving the highest discipline, but to sacrifice in any respect discipline for knowledge, is

giving the greater for the less, and is a sad mistake The main things with the ancient athlete were the suppleness of limb resulting from discipline, and the fixed purpose to run the race successfully. So with the young man stepping from scholastic to practical life, from the hand of his trainer to the open arena, the main question is not how much does he know, but rather, what facility has he acquired in the rapid, accurate and successful use of his mind, and with what spirit of high resolve does he enter the arena When the class in Greek recites to Professor Tyler, and the student has pronounced and translated till the Professor says " pause there," I doubt not the class will receive the same instruction in substance to-day, that you and I received fifteen, twenty or thirty years ago. Far otherwise is it in science. The instruction given and the theories advanced in science to-day have but slight kinship with what we were taught to believe twenty years ago. And the difference in scientific instruction is not so much in the fact that recent investigations have given more advanced ideas based on old fundamental principles, as it is that what we were taught to regard as fundamental and established have been swept away, and new foundations have been laid, to be in their turn ruthlessly torn up ; new theories are constantly battling with the old, and one wing of the scientific·host is ever sapping and mining in the vain effort to unsettle the deep foundations of the word of God, and one of the great questions to-day agitating the scientific world is whether the Bible account of the origin of man is true, or whether man is a derivative monkey. I would not be understood as being opposed to science or scientific instruction and pursuits ; far from it. I would encourage and foster them in due proportion, but regarding the college curriculum mainly as preparatory and disciplinary. I would give the sciences a subordinate position, and unhesitatingly maintain the ancient lan-

guages and mathematics in all the prominence of past times.
And when scientific men seek to overthrow the Bible, the
revealed will of God, by setting up in opposition to it the so-
called indisputable facts and deductions of science, I love to
remember that the strand of time through all the ages of the
past has ever been covered with the wrecks of what they have
called the unquestionable facts and the established deductions
of science.   And this must be so, for in the nature of the case,
all that the past has developed or sought to establish must yield
itself to the analysis of the last discovery and deduction, and so
on in an interminable series.   But the word of God was given
to us not by piece-meal and in detached portions, but it was
" once delivered to the Saints," aye, once for all, and it must and
will stand as the fundamental law of the universe until the dis-
cords and uncertainties of time merge into the harmonies and
certainties of eternity.

The presence of so goodly a number of the Alumni of the
North-West, in obedience to the summons of our Alma Mater
to join with the great family gathering in the golden jubilee at
the old hearthstone, testifies that we are one with you, brethren
of the East, in our devotion to Amherst College.

We have not come from an adjoining town or a neighboring
parish, with the old horse and family carriage.   The Amherst
Alumni of the North-West, with head-quarters at Chicago, are
scattered over a broad territory, and when we meet, there or
here, it is at some sacrifice.   Our altar-fires are kept burning
brightly, but it is at some cost.   From our churches, offices and
counting-rooms for hundreds of miles around, we came to head-
quarters and taking our drawing-rooms and hotels on wheels,
linked to a flaming chariot of fire, we have leaped the chasm of
a thousand miles intervening between the chief city of the
North-West and this mountain-bound, scholastic, beautiful jewel

of a New England village, and we are with you to-day in shouting the praises of Alma Mater. And I wish to say to our Eastern friends of the Alumni, that while there are differences and diversities in the different parts of the country and in the inhabitants of the various sections, still there is a great similarity in their general wants and necessities. What the North-West wants, aye, what the Nation wants to-day, is thought, not encyclopædias ; men of thorough discipline, rather than men of mere learning. Our broad and sparsely settled States are to be filled with the teeming millions of the coming time, and our cry to the old institutions of learning at the East is, at all hazards preserve in the college course the studies most conducive to discipline ; give us young men, (may I not say young women also ?) yes, give us young men and young women who have learned how to think ; men and women fitted to control because they have been themselves controlled : fitted to command because they have been taught to obey : men and women in whom are harmoniously blended the sternness of the most rigid thought, with the meekness of the spirit of the Gospel. Then shall we have men and women who can master facts as they meet them, and can grapple successfully with the living issues of practical life.

Some of you, my brethren, are bowed with years and the honors the world has thrust upon you—some are erect, elastic and full of the fire of youth, and some are rejoicing in the strength and success of middle life. But we all feel young to-day, for we have been living over our boyish days again, and we shall return to our homes with hearts warmer, pulses stronger, and aims higher than ever before. I know not how fully my experience may accord with yours, but engrossed with the cares and labors of my profession, I have been unable to prosecute the studies I pursued in College, and the definite facts that

·I learned have been largely forgotten. I suspect I should make an awkward appearance in a recitation room, and I know I could not pass an examination for admission to the next freshman class without much preparatory study. And yet I never have, nor do I to-day, count my college course as a failure or the time spent here as lost. On the contrary, all in my present experience that I cherish most sacredly had their beginnings in college days. Slight though it may be, still whatever of refined taste, of thirst for learning, of intellectual culture, of mental discipline, of high ambition, or of love to God have blessed my life, I owe, under God, to Amherst College. And in this glad hour of jubilee, I can join heartily with the warmest friend of the College in the hope that the achievements of the past fifty years may not satisfy our ambition, but that through all the coming years of our Republic, Amherst College may stand in the very front, doing valiant service for sound learning and an evangelical faith.

SPEECH OF GEORGE C. CLARKE, ESQ. .

Mr. President and Gentlemen of the Alumni:—It is to the accident of my being this year at the head of the Western Association of Alumni that I have the honor of this call. Many of you know something of this Association, and how each year the Amherst men living in the West gather together in a social reunion, to talk over college days, to meet classmates and friends, and to keep alive the love of old Amherst. We were perhaps the first in the West to establish these Alumni gatherings, and now all the colleges have their yearly reunions. But none are more largely attended, or more enthusiastic, or more successful than those of Amherst graduates. It is a pleasant thought that a thousand miles away from this college home in the new West which was a *terra incognita* in the boyhood days of many here, the children of Amherst should gather yearly to celebrate the praises of the Alma Mater.

I remember to have heard the late Joshua Giddings say that in the early part of his political life he was in one of the departments at Washington, when the news was brought of a fight and massacre at Chicago. No one connected with the department had ever heard the name before, or had the slightest idea of its location. There was a great hunting through maps, but no such settlement could be discovered. The party then adjourned to the war department, but found as great ignorance there. Fortunately, however, a new military map of the frontier ports displayed on closer examination, against a small river and fort on Lake Michigan, the, till then unknown name, "Chicago." This could not have been far from the year we to-day celebrate, of the birth of this foster mother of ours. I imagine if, at the ceremonies that may have attended that first birth celebration, some one should have been called to respond for Chicago, that there would have been as great astonishment and as little knowledge of its whereabouts as Joshua Giddings found at Washington. Doubtless, the audience would have looked with some expectation to see a red-skinned chief in feathers and war paint appear as the representative of the unknown settlement whose name proclaimed its probable inhabitants, yet to-day, after but fifty years, when some, perhaps, who stood on this spot on that inauguration day are mingling with us in celebrating this semi-centennial, among the most honored salutations is one to "Chicago," and the response comes from a score or more lawyers, preachers, merchants and teachers, claiming Chicago as their home and dear old Amherst as their Alma Mater.

If there is any ignorance now of the greatness of Chicago, it must be because its citizens, everywhere famed for modesty, so rarely, when abroad, mention its name or spread its praises.

It is often said that in these times we make history fast. But it seems to me we make geography faster. Take the maps of your childhood and see what you find in them west of the Alleghanies, and especially west of the Mississippi,—the great Indian territory, where now are the States of Kansas and Nebraska, and beyond, the vast trail of undivided country marked with the startling name, "The Great American Desert." Did you ever think you would traverse that trackless waste? And yet, doubtless there are some with us here who have crossed that fearful desert, not on camels backs, through miles of burning sand, but seated luxuriously in palace cars, driven over the iron rails of civilization—whisked past flourishing villages and towns, catching glimpses of churches, and schools and seminaries, to come here bringing birthday gifts in their hands and never-parting love in their hearts, to the old mother who fostered so tenderly their boyhood days, and I imagine that none of all her sons come with more eager longing to see the dear old place again, with a more filial devotion to the home and foster-mother of their youth, than those of us who went away from this beautiful home among the mountains, to live on the broad, flat prairies of the West. They say, you know, that the Swiss are the most patriotic and home-loving people of the world, and away from their native mountains, sometimes die of home-sickness. Whether mountains create patriotism, and why those who have lived among them seem to love their country most tenderly, to leave it with the most regret, to pine for it most earnestly, and to return to it most eagerly, are questions not to be discussed here. But if it is true that those sons among the hills love the home of their childhood with greatest affection,—it is equally true that those sons who, leaving their native hill-sides, spend the years of manhood on the flat plains, where neither mountain nor hill rises to break the dead monotony, but where there is seen but the uninviting level of the boundless plain, do long most home-sickly for the dear old hills that, as Ruskin says, "feed and gnaw and strengthen" the silent waves of the blue mountains lifted toward heaven in a stillness of perpetual mercy. I think I speak the hearts of many when I say, that when, in my western home, my thoughts go back to my old college home, and I call to memory the scenes of my college life, and the associations of college days, I do not think first or chiefly of these walls of brick, nor of classmates or teachers, but first and always, with never-failing love and tender recollection of those beautiful mountains in the south, of Holyoke and Tom and No-

19

notuck, of the sunny slopes of Pelham, over which you and
I have so often watched the clouds casting their swift morning
shadows,—of the range of western hills, looking toward which,
we have so often gazed with delight at the glorious splendor of
an Amherst sunset, the sky ablaze with gold, and those hills lit
up with a glory of light and color we can never forget.

What a teacher has been this glorious scenery of Amherst!
Giving all honor to faithful professors—there has been through
all these years a silent but most effective instructor in Nature
herself, instilling into the hearts and hands of the men privil-
eged to study here, lessons of beauty that have transformed
their character as much as the lessons in mathematics or classics
have cultivated the mind   Could any thoughtful man, with
a mind alive to beauty, pass daily along the winding walk on
the top of our college hill, and witness the beautiful landscape
spread out before him,—the semi-circular sweep of the Holyoke
range, the silvery billows of the Connecticut encircling the
mountains, the varied hues of the carpet-like meadows, the
white villages nestling in the hills, the ever changing colors in
the Pelham slopes,—could he witness all these scenes, and not
grow to be a better and a wiser man, with a larger heart and a
more beautiful character?

One of our most eloquent Alumni once said that in his college days he used to roam almost daily over these hills, and he
thought he knew every pine cone on the wooded hights.   How
much of the passionate yet tender love of nature that breathes
through all his words, and that makes those who listen to him,
love the grass and flowers and trees with a wonderful new love
unknown before—how much of this he owes to his four years of
Amherst life, I know not, but I think he would confess that the
chief inspiration came during his college days.   And to most of
us nature was not altogether mute; we had a grand old teacher,

who spent his life in turning over the rocky leaves of nature's book and tracing with reverent hand and eye the record God had written there. He never feared that he should find in the words the Almighty had written in the rocks, a contradiction of the truths He had given in His word, and while He taught us all to search and study the mysterious characters written in nature's book, he turned our eyes with reverence to the Creator, whose words are always truth, and, to quote from a classmate's song :—

> That reverend sage, who loved to trace
> Creation through the rocks ;
> And on the rocky ages place
> His academic blocks.
> O, the grandest man of men, good sirs !
> In the days when we were boys,
> Held royal reign, sir, heart and brain,
> In the days when we were boys.

Keep on, O faithful instructors of our lessons of poetry and philosophy, of history and mathematics and classics, but fail not to teach your pupils to read the lessons written in the petals of flowers, the rocky ledges of your iron shores, the gems gathered from the depths of earth, and the mysterious metals dropped from the starry world. Then shall you send forth men, not only with minds matured and cultivated by intelligent efforts, but with hearts elevated and filled with beauty, to ennoble and purify and bless the world in which they are to mingle.

LETTER FROM DR. STORRS, READ BY MR. BEECHER.

"BATHS OF LUCCA," June 23, 1871.

My Dear Dr. Stearns:—It is as charming and brilliant a morning in this delightful Italian valley as June ever brings to you on the Connecticut; the air full of temperate warmth, the vast and vivid blue arch above unspotted by a cloud, the luxuriant hills and the swift and shining emerald river rejoicing together in the perfect splendor of the universal sunshine. As I sit by the window, after breakfast, and look upon the landscape which recent rains have washed and refreshed, and which the sun is now transfiguring, my thoughts go back to the similar mornings which I have rejoiced in, in other days, on the Amherst hills; and I find myself wondering whether this 23d of June is—or is to be, when it reaches you—as lovely and glorious on your side of the water, as it is on this; and whether your distant western horizon will be radinat to-night with as superb a sunset as those which used often to entrance our eyes between 1835 and 1839. And so I am reminded still further that two or three weeks hence you will be celebrating the fiftieth anniversary of the College, whose eighteenth anniversary was one of the memorable days of my life.

If this should reach you, as I hardly suppose that it will, before your Commencement, will you be kind enough to present for me to the members of the Board, and to the gentlemen of the Faculty, my greetings and congratulations on the occasion so full of interest to them all, and the assurance of my warm personal regard. And if there should be anywhere an unoccupied crevice in the series of the exercises at the meeting of the Alumni, where a distant voice may for an instant make itself heard, without interruption to those on the ground, will you present my "hail" and "God-speed" to all the graduates, with the assurance that a college like ours, fresh, vigorous, liberal, evangelical, wide in its range, high in its aims, and quickening in its spiritual force, never looks so noble, or so bright and rich in its promises of good, as when one looks back to it from under the dense though lifting shadows that still brood over Italy. I set it beside the college of the Propaganda, which lately fronted me for six weeks at Rome, or beside the other wholly secularized institutes in the same city, where learning is irreligious, and science atheistic—and I see that our whole distinctive, prophetic, American civilization, in which the future of the world is involved, has its germs and its guaranties in just such institutions. God long preserve, and still enlarge them, till the earth is full of their light and power!

R. S. Storrs, Jr.

Printed in Dunstable, United Kingdom